Preschool

Big Fun Workbook!

AaBb Cc Dd Ee
Ff Gg Hh Ii Jj Kk
Ll Mm Nn Oo Pp
Qq Rr Ss Tt Uu
Vv Ww Xx Yy Zz

MW00886086

Ready for Big Fun?

This jumbo educational workbook is filled with hundreds of teacher-approved activities & puzzles to help your preschooler enjoy learning about the alphabet, sight words, colors, shapes, numbers, sizes, patterns, counting, opposites, and early math concepts.

How to use this book:

1 **Choose the right time.**
Start new activities when she's well rested, and fed.

2 **Allow your child to take the lead.**
Let your child select the activities of their interest, and do them at a pace that works for them.

3 **Stay close by.**
Sit nearby so you'll be right there to guide her if needed.

4 **Praise, praise, praise!**
Acknowledge her efforts enthusiastically after completing each page.

5 **Be patient!**
If you see your child struggling with a concept, maintain patience, give clues, but don't provide answers.

SCHOOL TIMETABLE

Hour	Monday		Wednesday	Thursday	Friday

This Book
Belongs To

TABLE OF CONTENTS

This is Me!

I have_____ color 👀

and_____ color

Color in the Alphabet
Upper Case

A B C D E

F G H I J K

L M N O P

Q R S T U

V W X Y Z

Aa Bb Cc Dd

Ee Ff Gg Hh

Ii Jj Kk Ll

Mm Nn Oo

Pp Qq Rr Ss

Tt Uu Vv Ww

Xx Yy Zz

Prewriting practice

Directions: Trace the lines to put the bow on the gift.

Prewriting practice

Directions: Trace the lines to put the chocolate heart on top of the cupcake.

Hopping bunny race

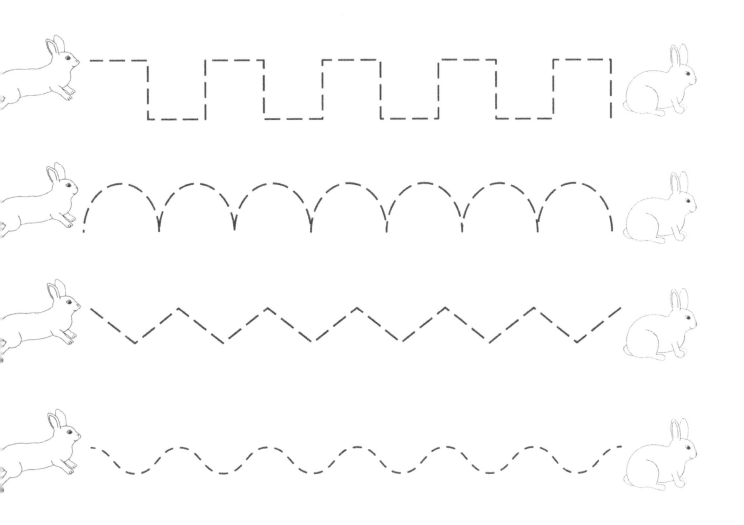

Hopping bunny race

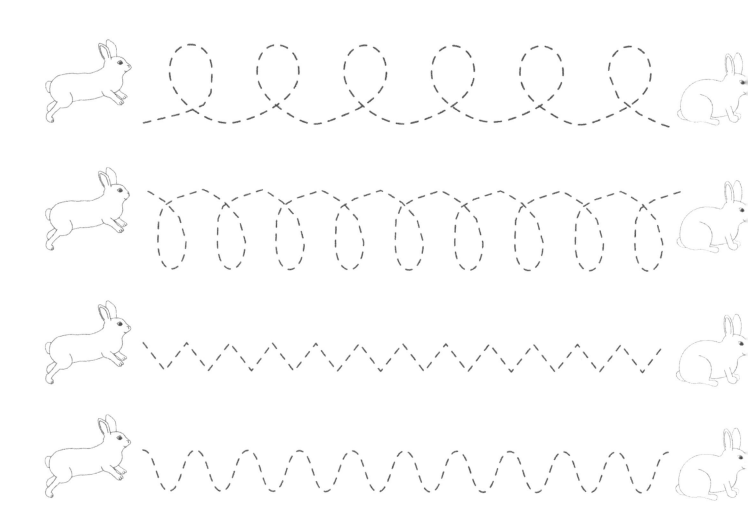

Dash Trace Handwriting
Lowercase Letters

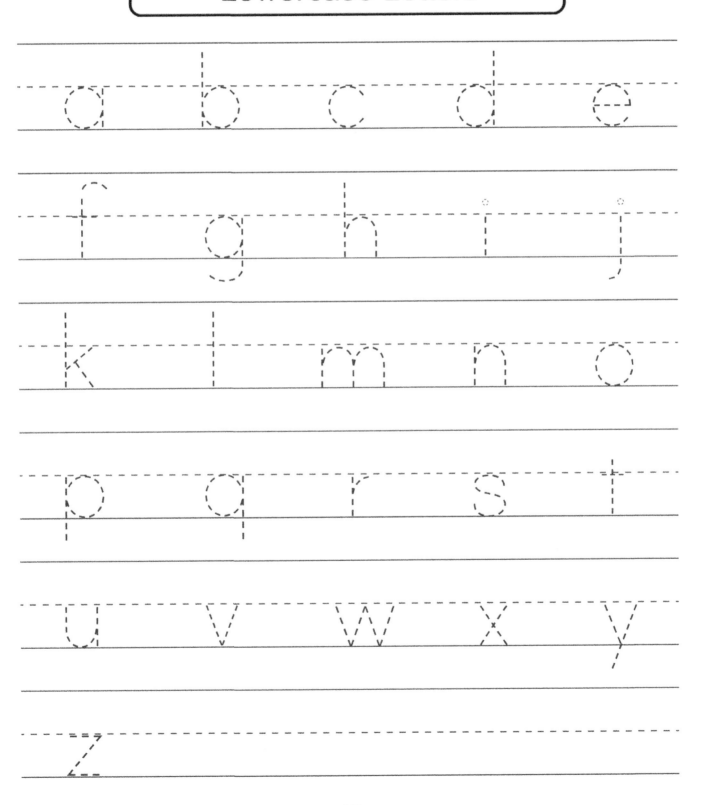

Handwriting Practice
Uppercase Letters

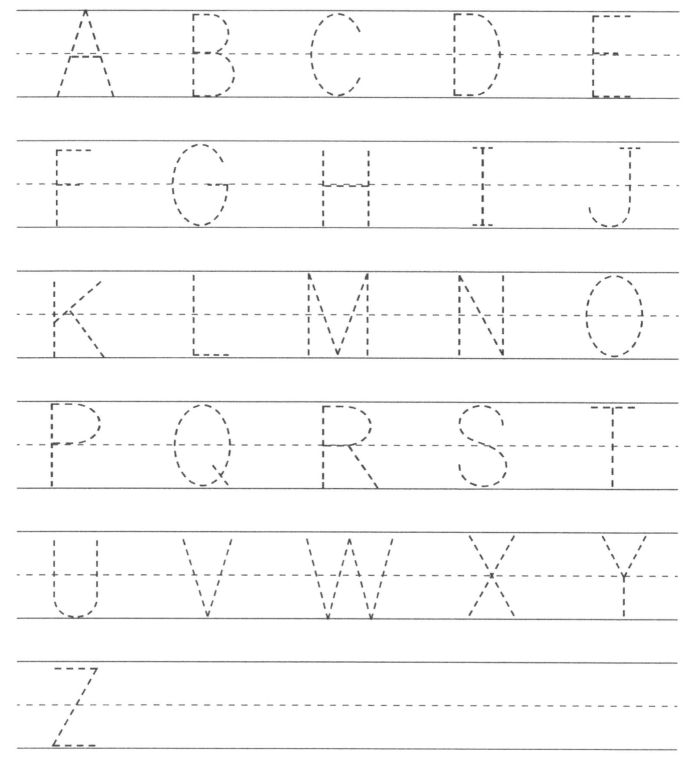

Blank Writing Practice

Blank Writing Practice

Alphabet Letters A - Z

Color

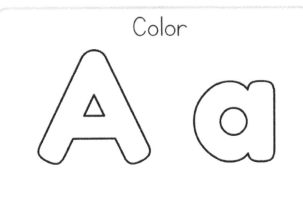

Color

Apple

Circle it

b A a i I A a C q

H a E A K a Z a

A a N o a I q d

Trace   Write

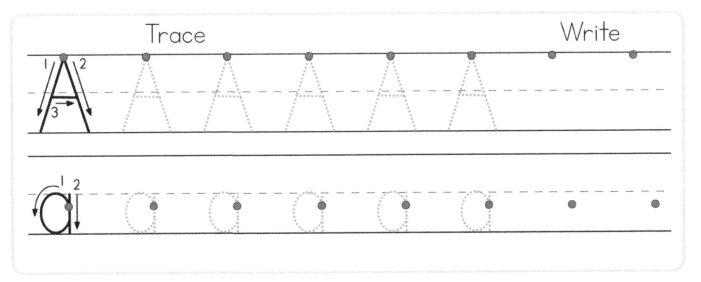

A - B - C -

-D - E - F -

-G - H - I -

Trace

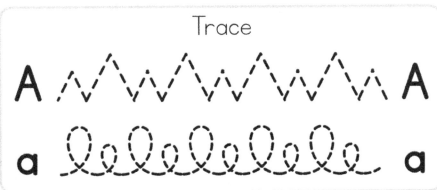

17

Alphabet Letters A - Z

Color

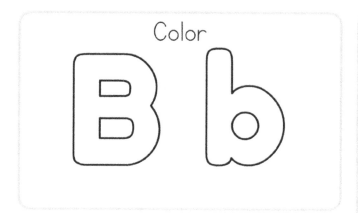

Color

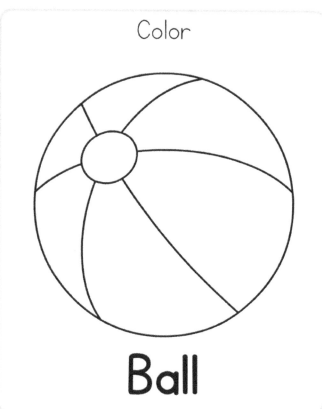

Ball

Circle it

a b R d P p B a
B p R b c B d b
b B c B a q b g

Trace   Write

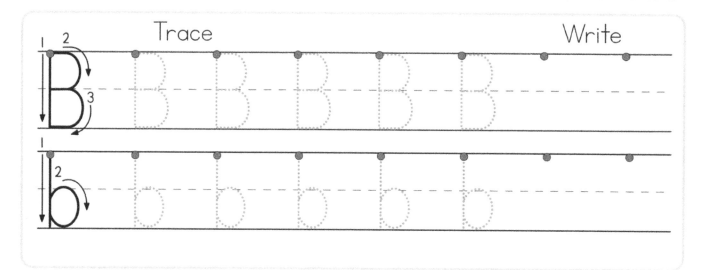

A - B - C -
-D - E - F -
-G - H - I -

Trace

B Q Q Q Q Q Q Q Q Q B
b l l l l l l l l l b

Alphabet Letters A - Z

Color

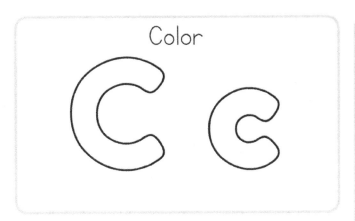

Color

Cat

Circle it

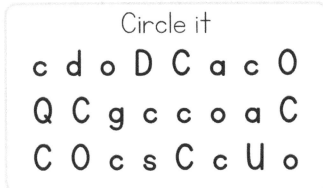

c d o D C a c O
Q C g c c o a C
C O c s C c U o

Trace   Write

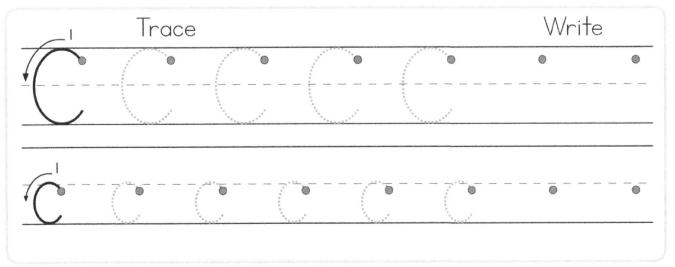

A - B - **C** -
- D - E - F -
- G - H - I -

Trace

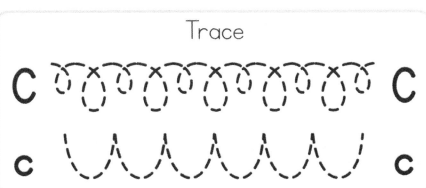

Alphabet Letters A - Z

Color

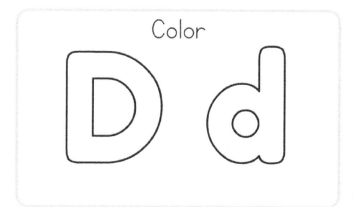

Color

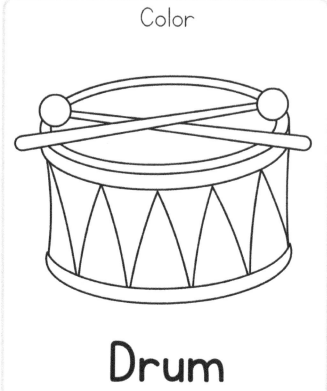

Drum

Circle it

O d b p D B d b
d O p D a D q d
q d O D d p O D

Trace

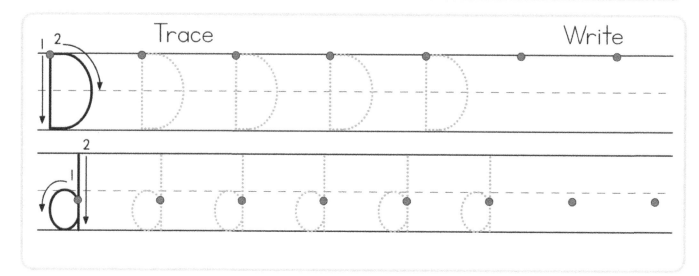

Write

A - B - C -
- D - E - F -
- G - H - I -

Trace

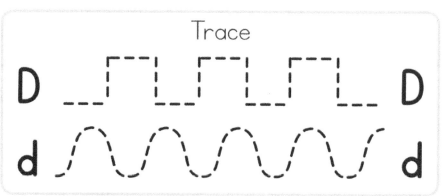

D   D
d   d

20

Alphabet Letters A - Z

Color

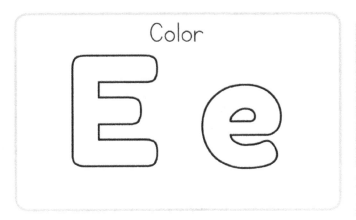

Color

Elephant

Circle it

E F e s o E H e
B e e E s F E o
e F o E E H e s

Trace   Write

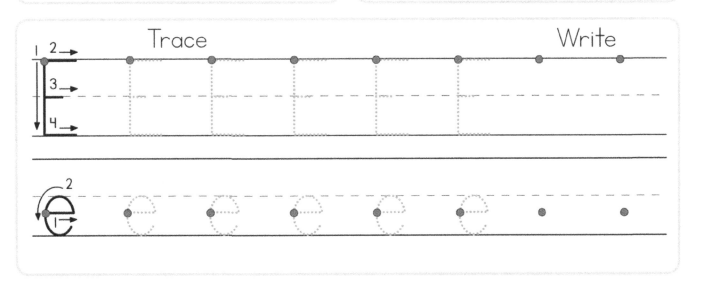

A - B - C -
- D - E - F -
- G - H - I -

Trace

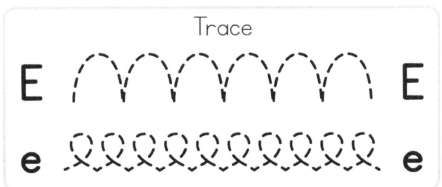

E

E

e

e

21

Alphabet Letters A - Z

Color

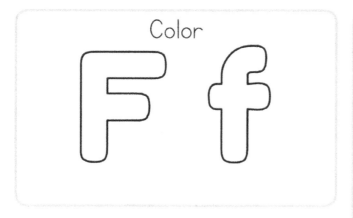

Color

Flower

Circle it

f E F t h f H F
t f H F k h F F
f f E h F t H f

Trace   Write

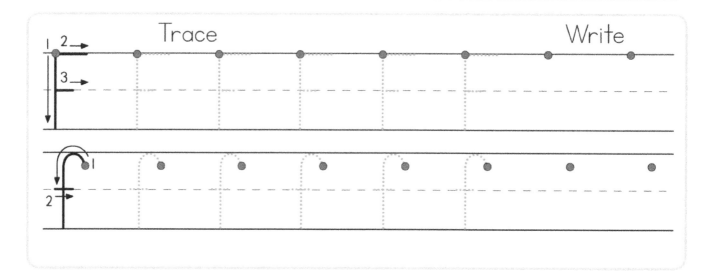

A - B - C -
- D - E - F -
- G - H - I -

Trace

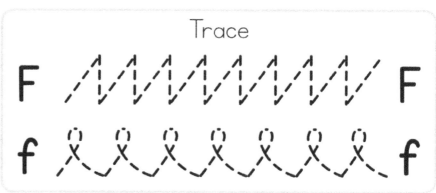

22

Alphabet Letters A - Z

Color

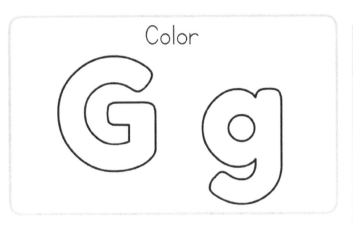

Color

Goat

Circle it

q G p g O q g G
O g C G G q g g
g G q C p g C Q

Trace   Write

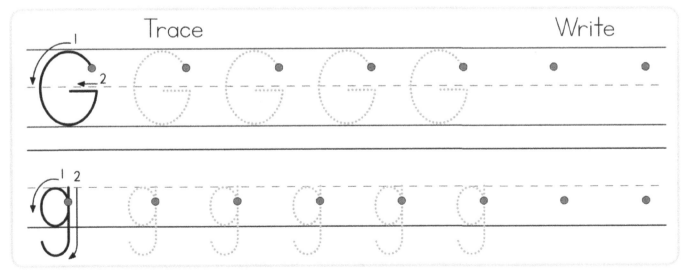

- D - E - F -
- G - H - I -
- J - K - L -

Trace

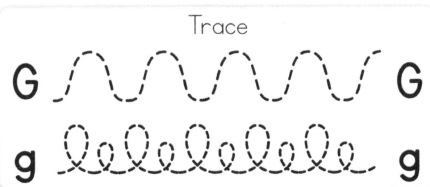

Alphabet Letters A - Z

Color

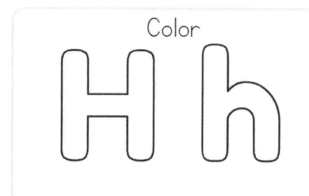

Color

Home

Circle it

h H k h n H N h
k h N H E h n H
H h E k h n H N

Trace

Write

Trace

- D - E - F -
- G - H - I -
- J - K - L -

H   H
h   h

Alphabet Letters A - Z

Color

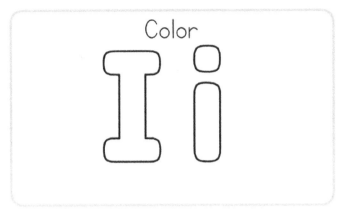

Color

Island

Circle it

Trace   Write

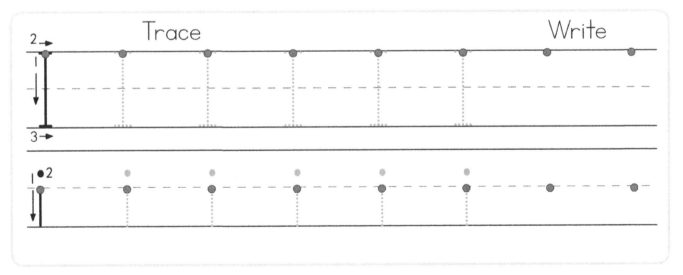

-D-E-F-
-G-H-**I**-
-J-K-L-

Trace

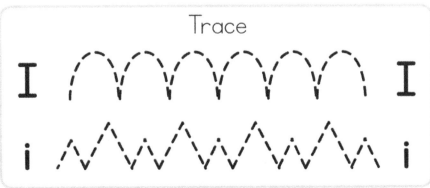

25

Alphabet Letters A - Z

Color

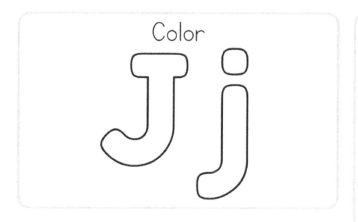

Color

Jam

Circle it

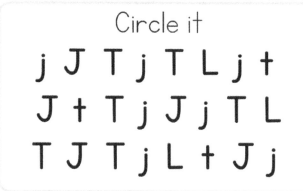

j J T j T L j t
J t T j J j T L
T J T j L t J j

Trace   Write

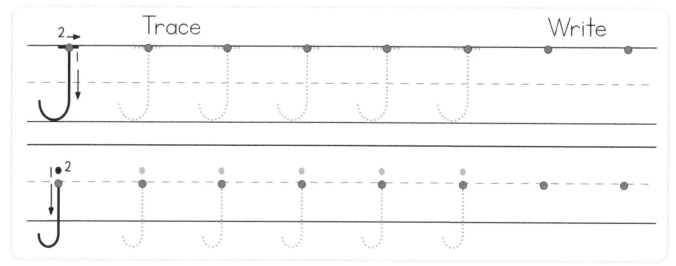

- G - H - I -
- **J** - K - L -
- M - N - O -

Trace

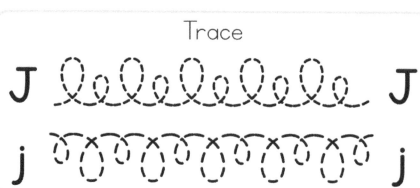

Alphabet Letters A - Z

Color

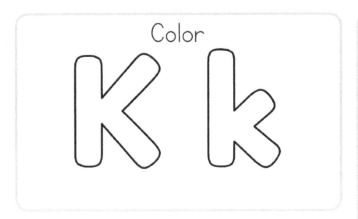

Color

Kite

Circle it

k K h k F x K X
F k x K k K h E
k X K F k h x K

Trace   Write

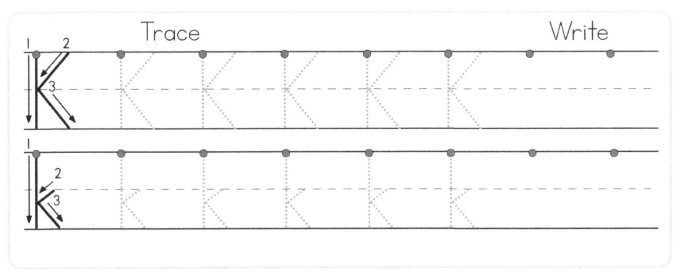

-G-H-I-
-J-K-L-
-M-N-O-

Trace

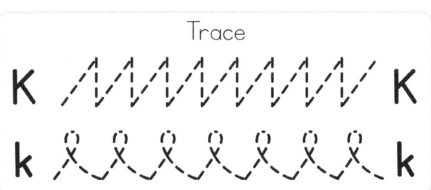

K   K

k   k

Alphabet Letters A - Z

Color

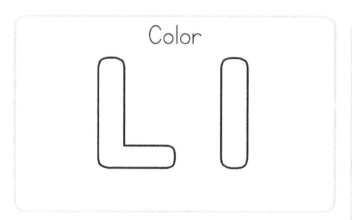

Color

Lemon

Circle it

L F l i H L l J

I L i V L t l j

F j l H j L I L

Trace   Write

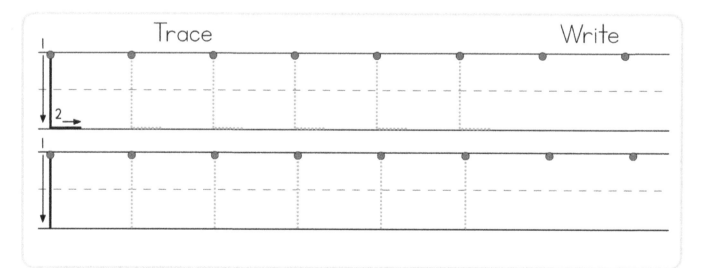

-G - H - I -

-J - K - L -

-M - N - O -

Trace

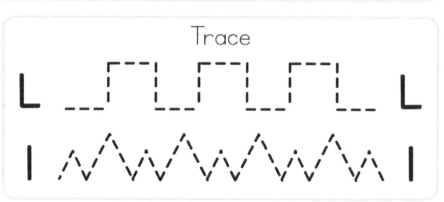

28

Alphabet Letters A - Z

Color

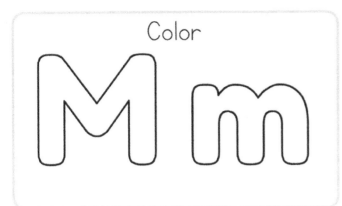

Color

Monkey

Circle it

m n M N m M w
m M w N W n m
N m W M n M m

Trace   Write

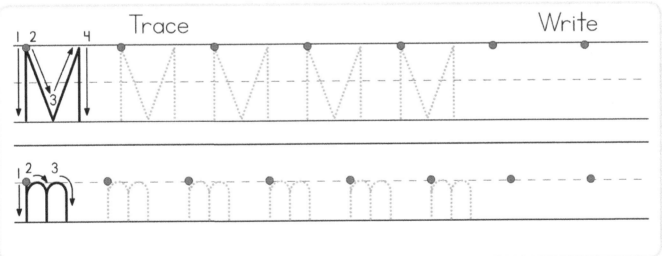

-J-K-L-
-M-N-O-
-P-Q-R-

Trace

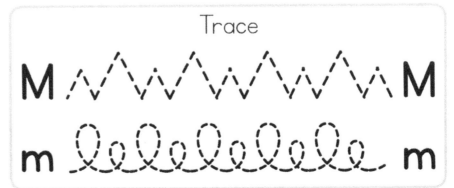

Alphabet Letters A - Z

Color

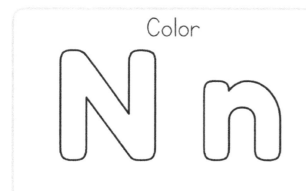

Color

Night

Circle it

M n h N H n N u
n N u h H n N h
N h n M N n u H

Trace

Write

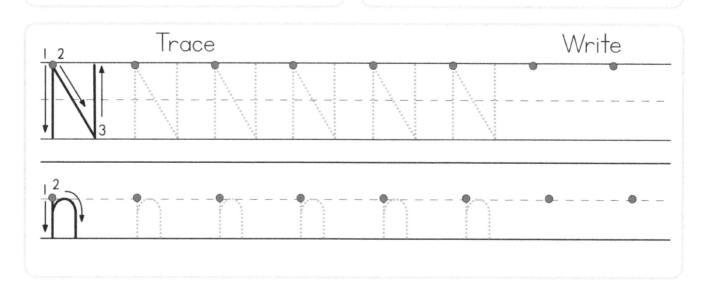

-J-K-L-
-M-N-O-
-P-Q-R-

Trace

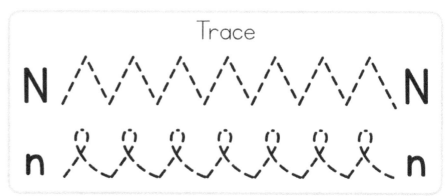

N ∧∧∧∧∧∧ N

n n

Alphabet Letters A - Z

Color

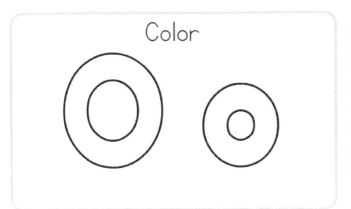

Color

Owl

Circle it

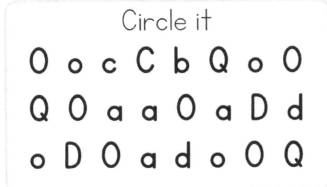

Trace   Write

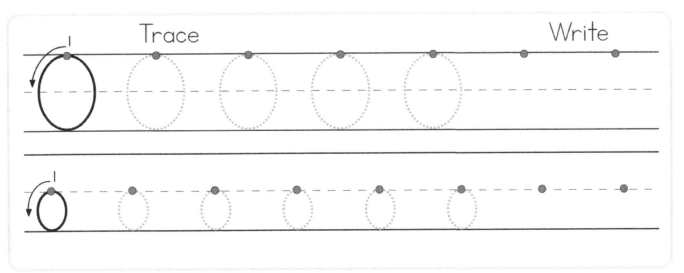

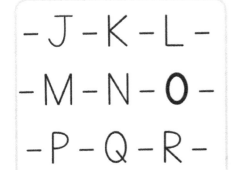

-J-K-L-
-M-N-O-
-P-Q-R-

Trace

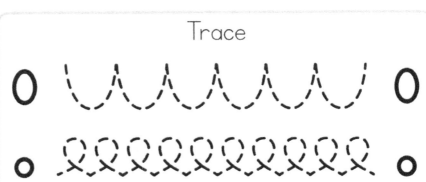

Alphabet Letters A - Z

Color

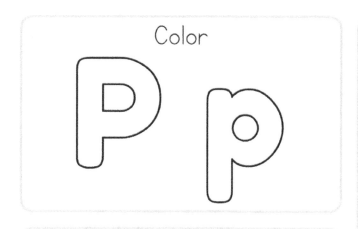

Color

Pig

Circle it

p P b p B b d P
b B p P b P B p
p P d p b p P d

Trace   Write

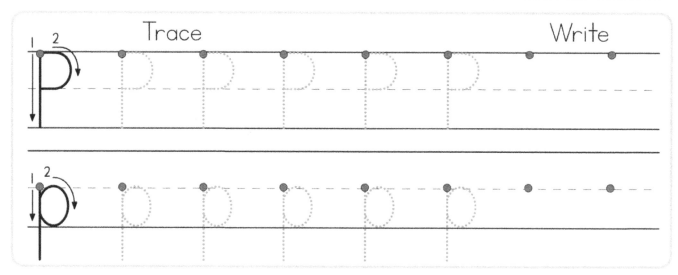

-M-N-O-
-P-Q-R-
-S-T-U-

Trace

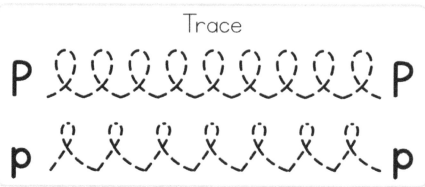

Alphabet Letters A - Z

Color

Color

Queen

Circle it

Q O q g q Q C q
O q Q g q C q Q
q p Q O Q g C q

Trace   Write

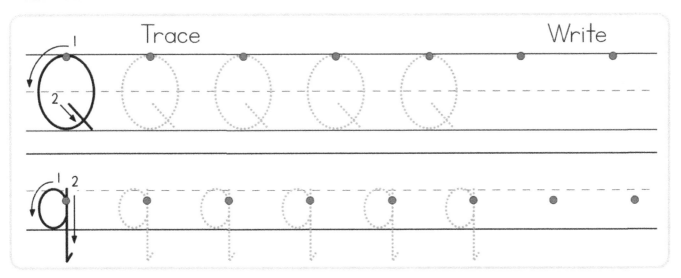

-M-N-O-
-P-Q-R-
-S-T-U-

Trace

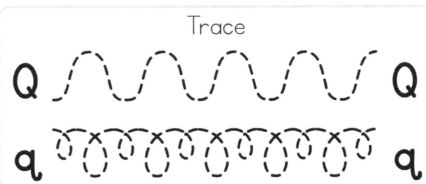

33

Alphabet Letters A - Z

Color

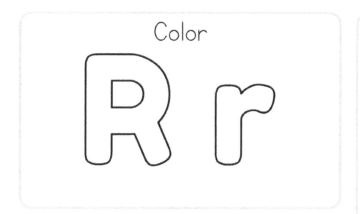

Color

Reindeer

Circle it

r R r n B R P r
r r P R R n r P
n R P r n B r R

Trace   Write

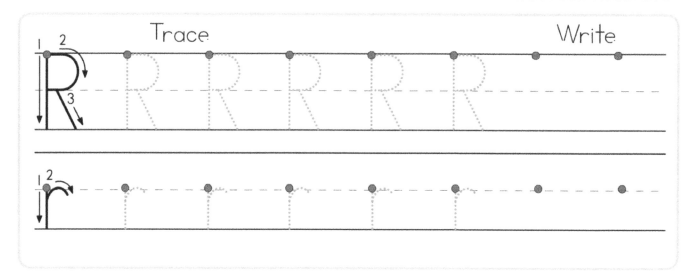

- M - N - O -
- P - Q - R -
- S - T - U -

Trace

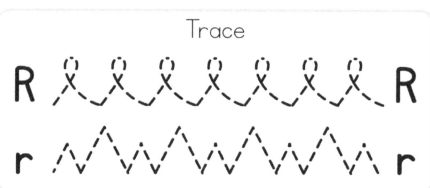

34

Alphabet Letters A - Z

Color

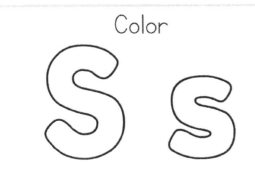

Color

Snake

Circle it

S e s Z s S z G
Z S C e z S s z
S e s G S s C s

Trace
Write

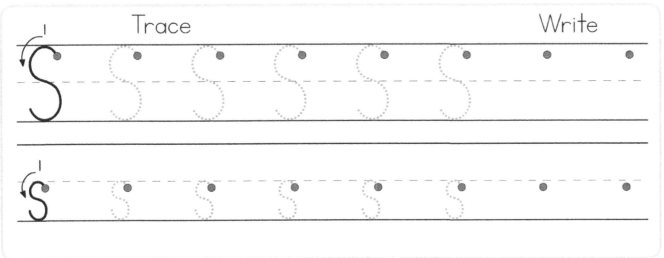

-P - Q - R -
-S - T - U -
-V - W - X -

Trace

S
S

S
s

Alphabet Letters A - Z

Color

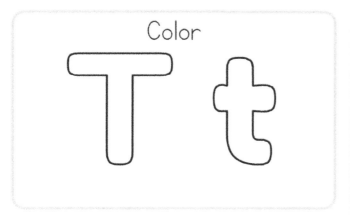

Circle it

t J I T F t f T
f t T J t L T J
T t J L I T t F

Color

Turkey

Trace · · · · · · · · · · Write

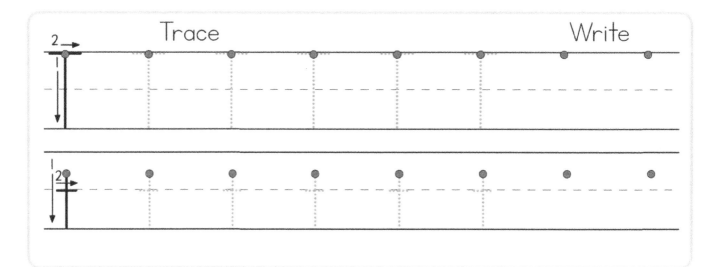

-P-Q-R-
-S-T-U-
-V-W-X-

Trace

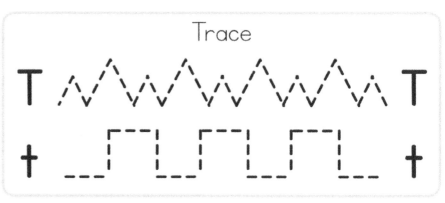

Alphabet Letters A - Z

Color

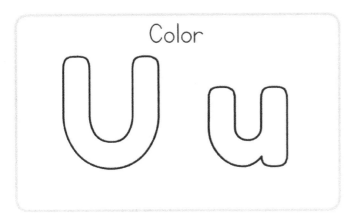

Color

Unicorn

Circle it

n U V u N n U u
U u v N V u U N
u N u U v u V U

Trace   Write

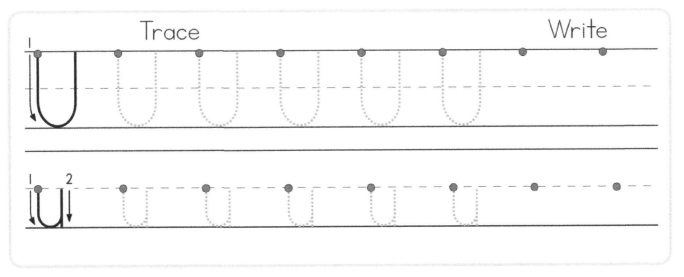

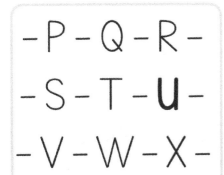

-P - Q - R -
-S - T - U -
-V - W - X -

Trace

u ∪∪∪∪∪∪∪ u

u ℓℓℓℓℓℓℓℓℓℓ u

37

Alphabet Letters A - Z

Color

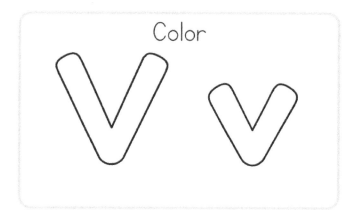

Circle it

U V n v N n v V
N v u V v U V N
u V U v u V v n

Color

Volcano

Trace   Write

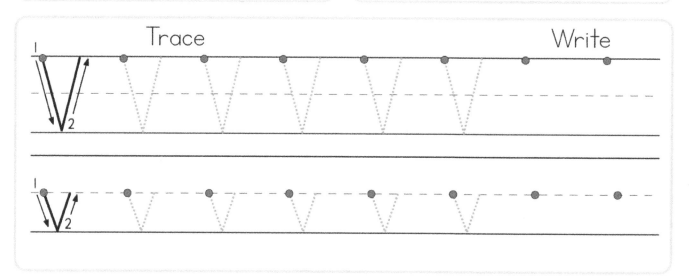

-S-T-U-
-V-W-X-
-Y-Z

Trace

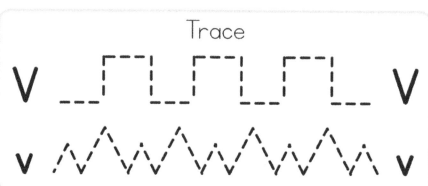

Alphabet Letters A - Z

Color

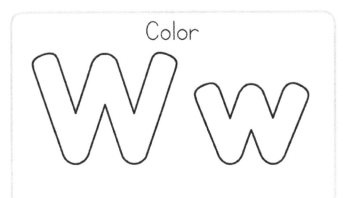

Color

Whale

Circle it

M W V w m W v
m v W M w V w
M w v m V W w

Trace   Write

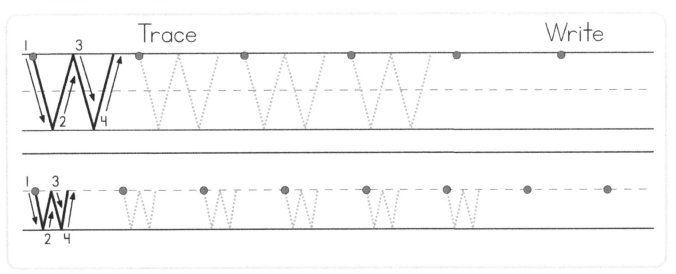

-S-T-U-
-V-W-X-
-Y-Z

Trace

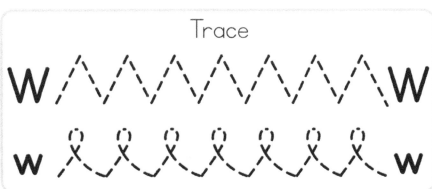

Alphabet Letters A - Z

Color

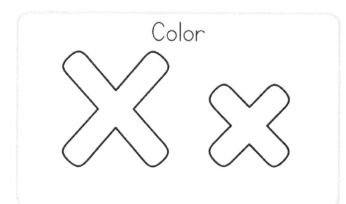

Color

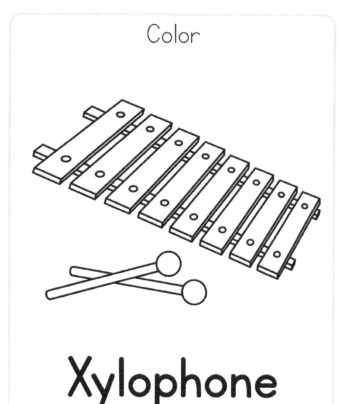

Circle it

V x X k K x V X
k x K V X v x X
X v x k V x K X

Xylophone

Trace   Write

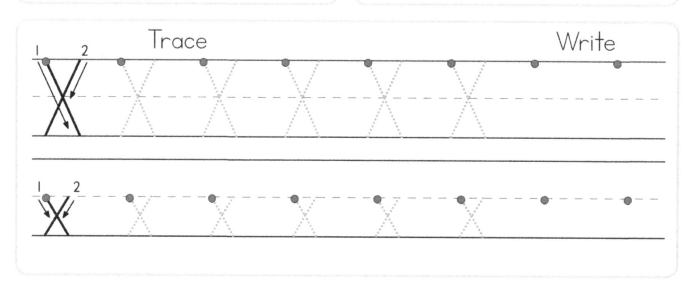

- S - T - U -
- V - W - **X** -
  - Y - Z

Trace

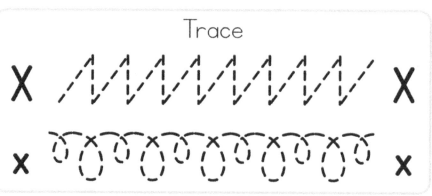

Alphabet Letters A - Z

Color

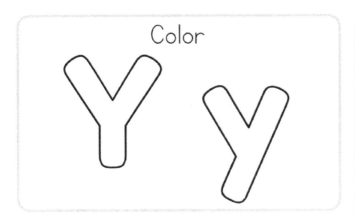

Color

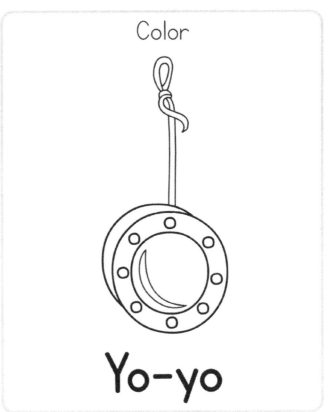

Yo-yo

Circle it

v Y U y X V Y y

y X Y u x y V Y

Y X y Y U x y V

Trace   Write

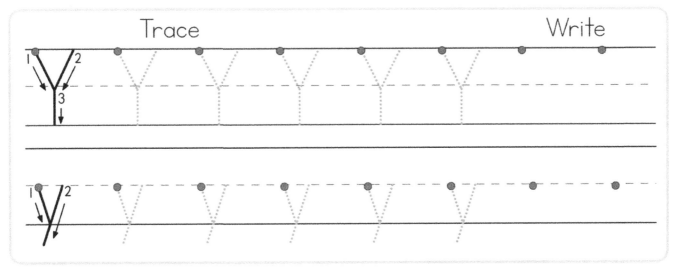

- S - T - U -
- V - W - X -
- Y - Z

Trace

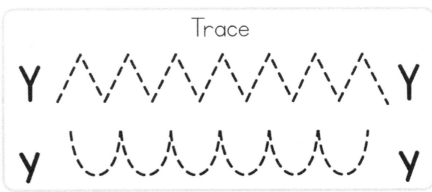

Alphabet Letters A - Z

Color

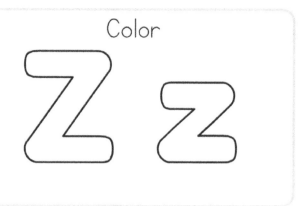

Color

Zebra

Circle it

z Z z s N Z z S

n Z S z n u Z z

Z N z S z Z u N

Trace   Write

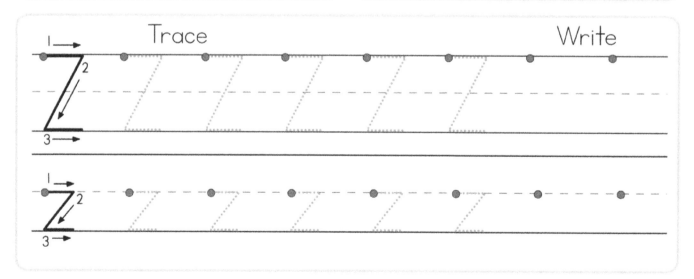

- S - T - U -

- V - W - X -

- Y - Z

Trace

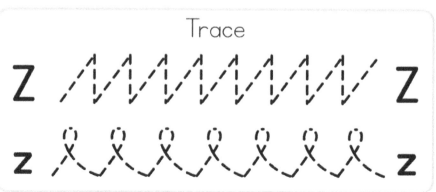

Sight Words
Let's Learn the Word "have"

have

Do you have a cat?

1. Trace the word.

have   have   have

2. Circle the word in the sentences.

What do you have?

I have to go home.

3. Finish the sentence below.

I _____ a nice bike.

Sight Words
Let's Learn the Word "are"

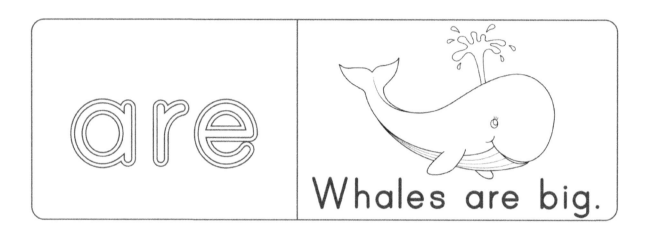

Whales are big.

1. Trace the word.

are   are   are   are

2. Circle the word in the sentences.

You are tall.

Flowers are pretty.

3. Finish the sentence below.

Ants   small.

Sight Words
three

Color it!

three

Trace it!

three

Write it!

Connect the letters!

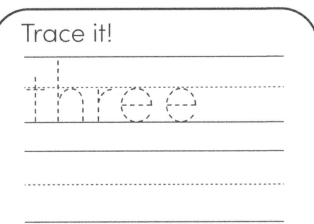
t o r e b
w h p s e

I have _____ dogs.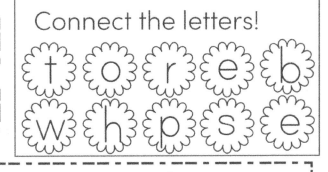

Find and color it!

there   three

this   three   there

their   the   three   that

Sight Words
Let's Learn the Word "eat"

Cows eat grass.

1. Trace the word.

eat eat eat eat

2. Circle the word in the sentences.

Do you eat vegetables?

Can you eat this?

3. Finish the sentence below.

Did you _____ lunch?

Sight Words
Let's Learn the Word "do"

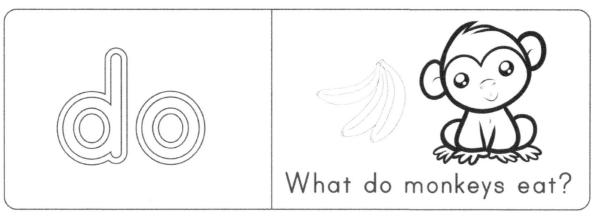

What do monkeys eat?

1. Trace the word.

do   do   do   do

2. Circle the word in the sentences.

What do you like?

I have to do homework.

3. Finish the sentence below.

What   you need?

Sight Words

can   can can can

and   and and and

Let's put them in sentences!

I _____ run fast.

Mom _____ dad went
to work.

Color in the Numbers

1 2 3 4 5

6 7 8 9 10

Number

1

Number Word

one

Trace and Write

1 1 1 1 1

Number Line

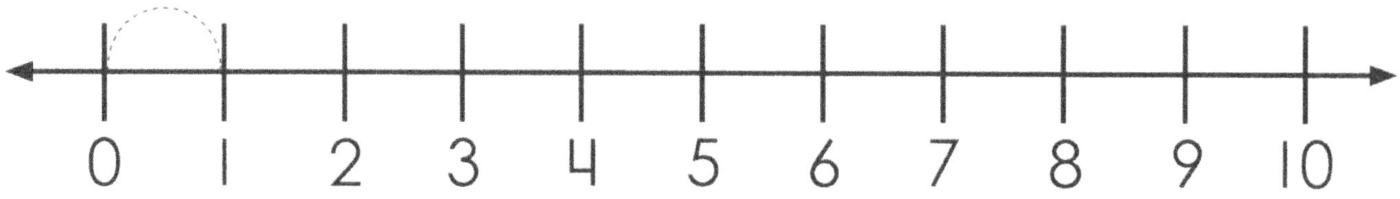

0
1
2
3
4
5
6
7
8
9
10

Ten Frame

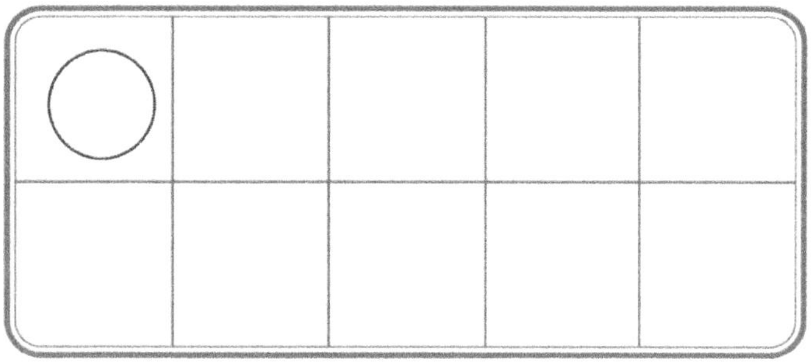

Dice

Tally Marks

Circle 1 Finger

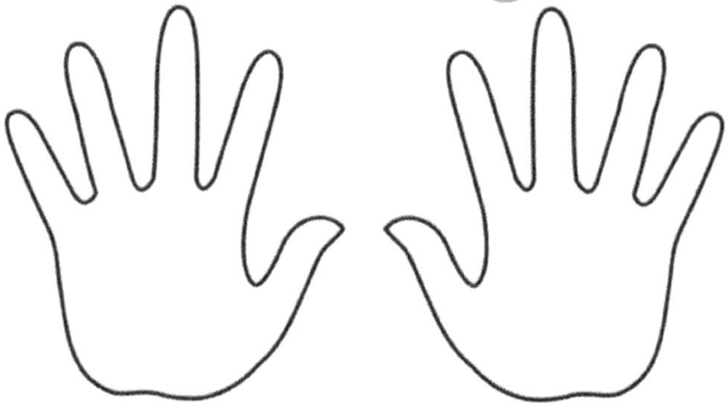

Number

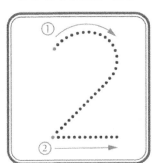

Number Word

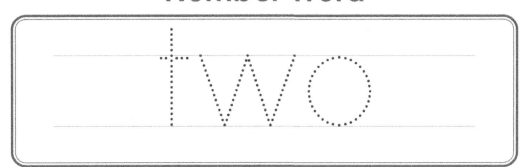

Trace and Write

Number Line

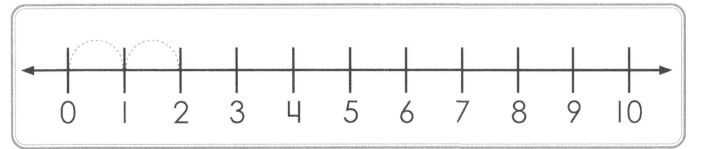

Ten Frame

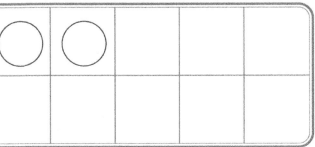

Dice

Tally Marks

Circle 2 Fingers

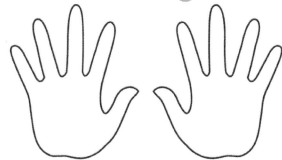

Number

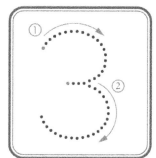

Number Word

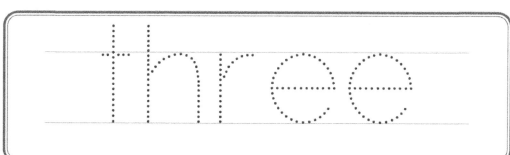

Trace and Write

Number Line

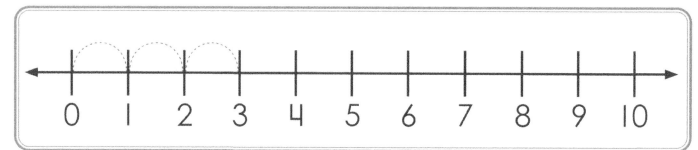

Ten Frame

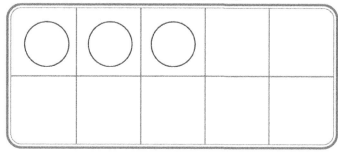

Dice

Tally Marks

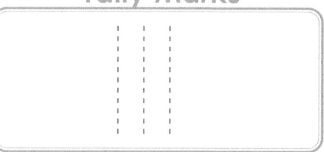

Circle 3 Fingers

Number

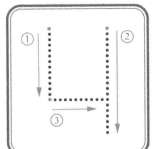

Number Word

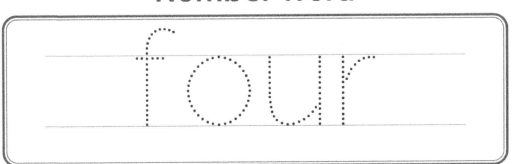

Trace and Write

Number Line

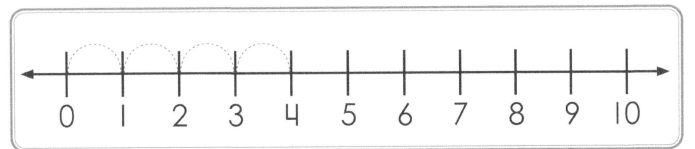

Ten Frame

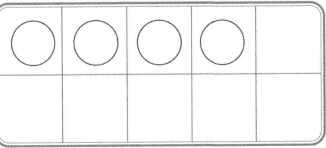

Dice

Tally Marks

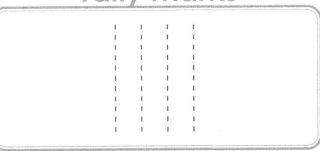

Circle 4 Fingers

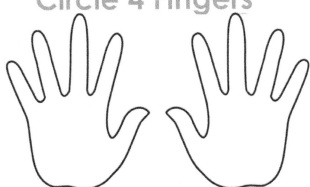

53

Number

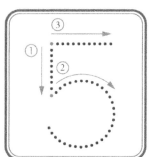

Number Word

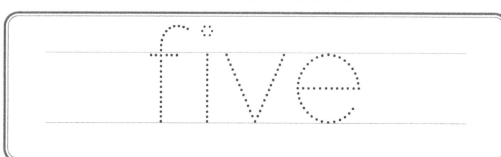

Trace and Write

Number Line

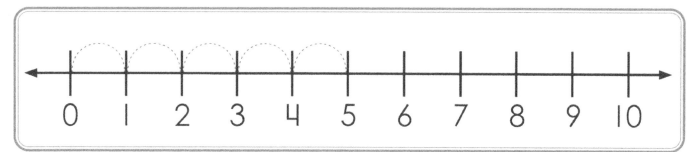

Ten Frame

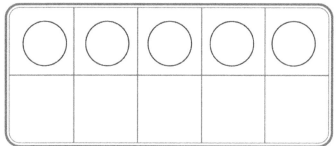

Dice

Tally Marks

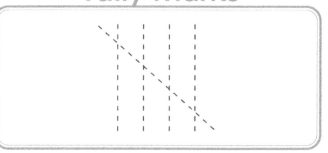

Circle 5 Fingers

54

Number

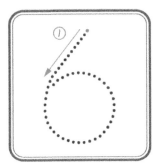

Number Word

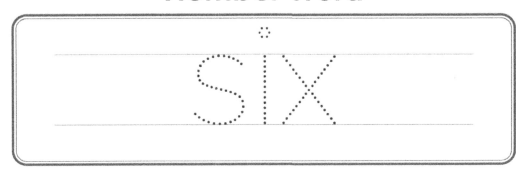

Trace and Write

Number Line

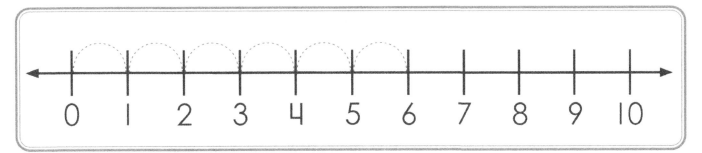

Ten Frame

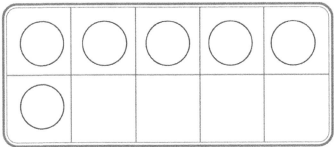

Dice

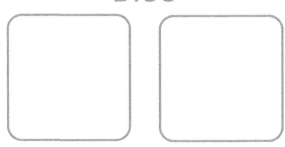

Tally Marks

Circle 6 Fingers

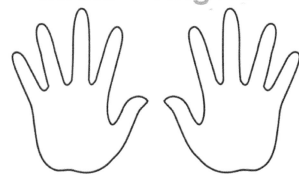

Number

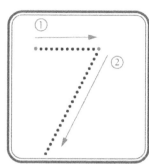

Number Word

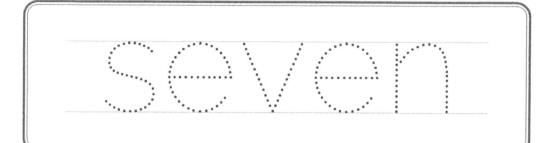

Trace and Write

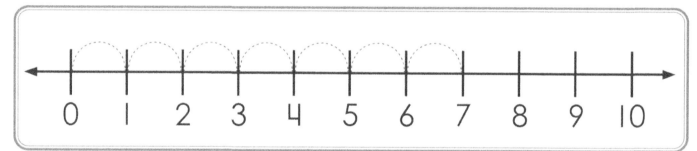

Number Line

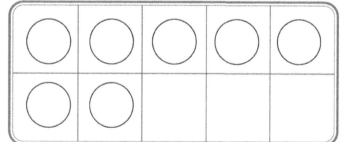

Ten Frame

Dice

Tally Marks

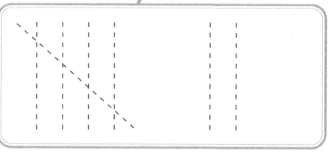

Circle 7 Fingers

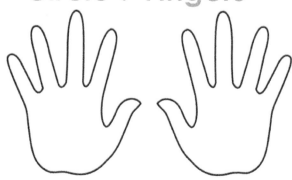

56

Number

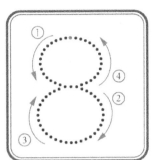

Number Word

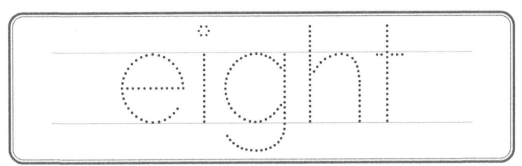

Trace and Write

Number Line

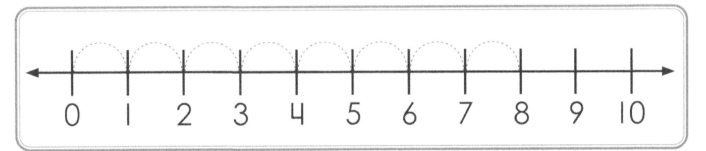

Ten Frame

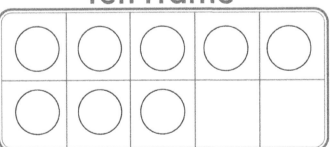

Dice

Tally Marks

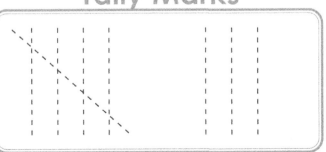

Circle 8 Fingers

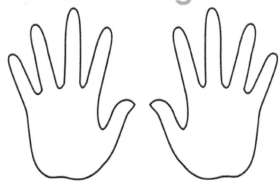

57

Number

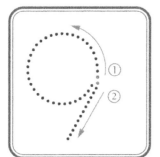

Number Word

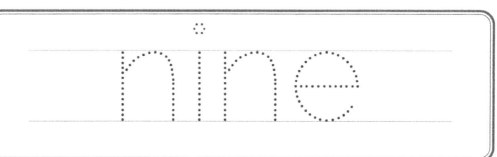

Trace and Write

Number Line

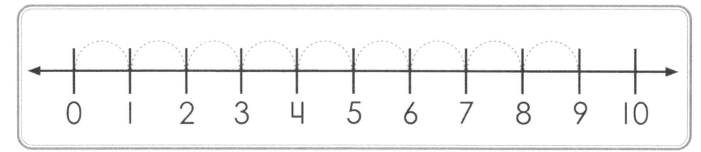

Ten Frame

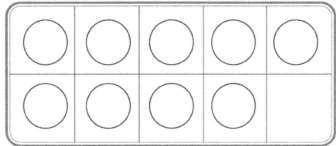

Dice

Tally Marks

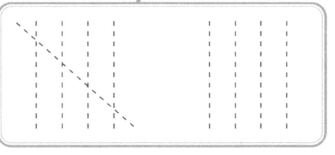

Circle 9 Fingers

Number

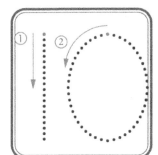

Number Word

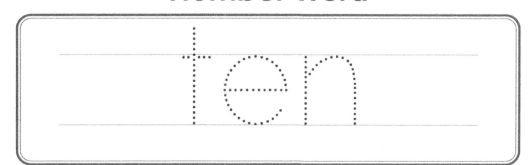

Trace and Write

Number Line

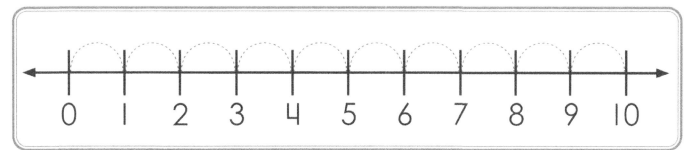

Ten Frame

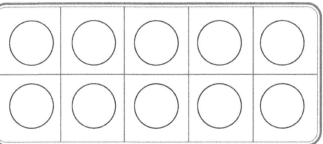

Dice

Tally Marks

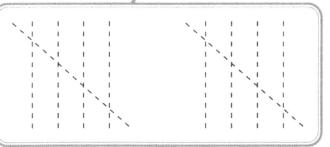

Circle 10 Fingers

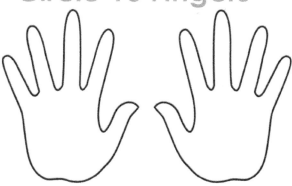

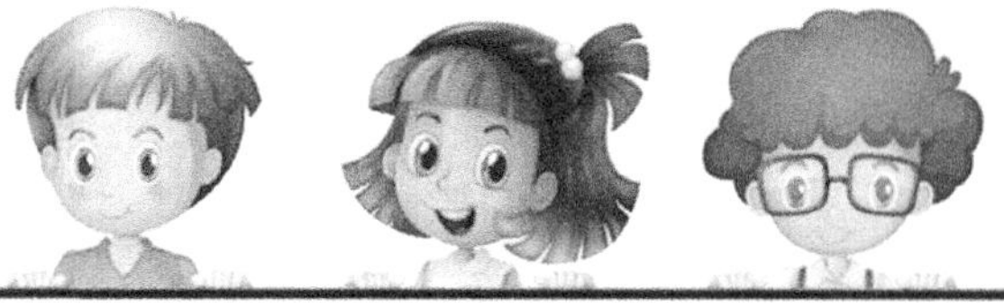

Numbers

1	1	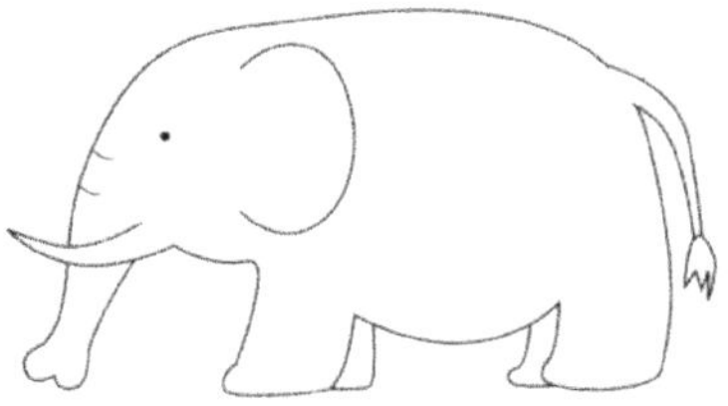
2	2	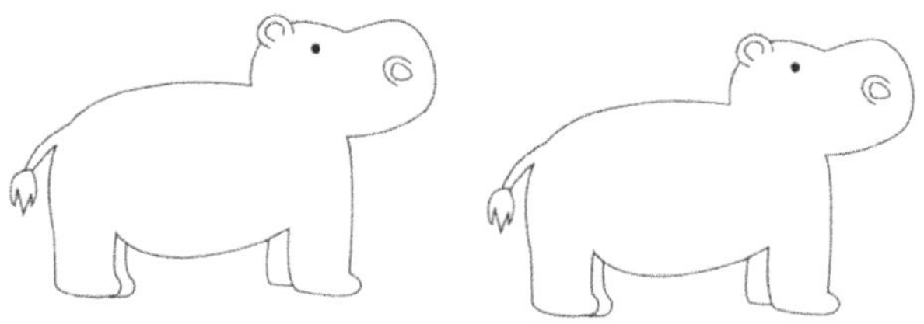
3	3	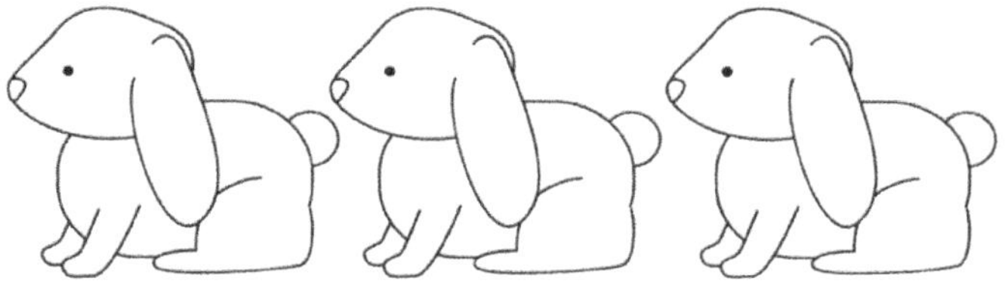
4	4	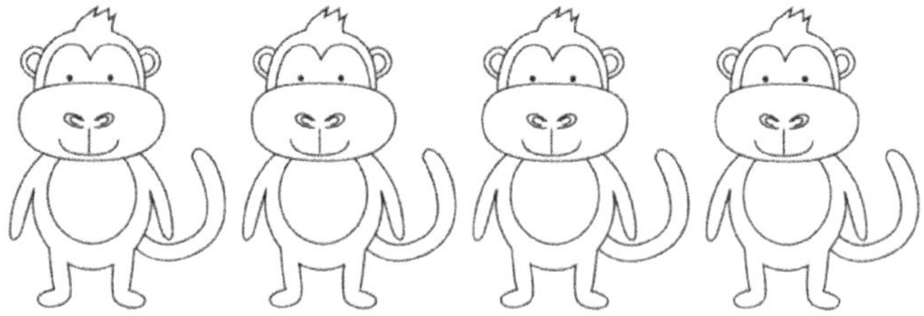
5	5	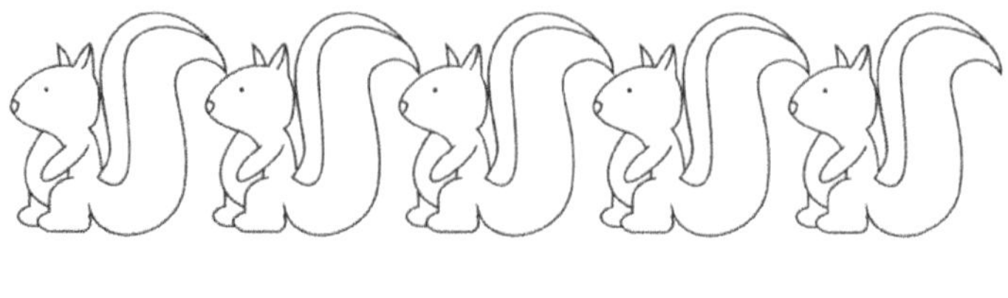

number matching

Directions: Count the pictures. Then match them with numbers.

1

5

2

4

3

number matching

Directions: Count the pictures. Then match them with numbers.

Counting

Directions: Read the number. Then circle the correct amount of objects.

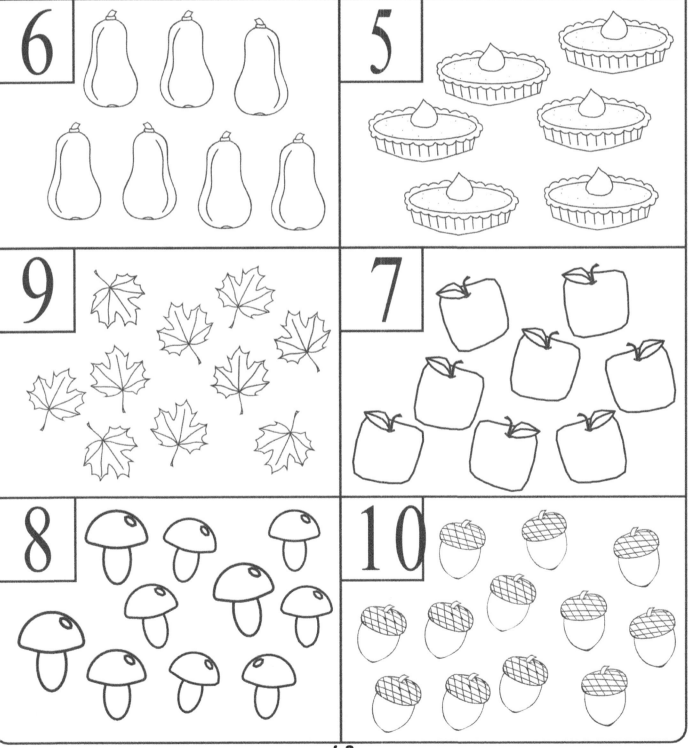

Counting

Directions: Count the pictures in each box. Then color the correct number.

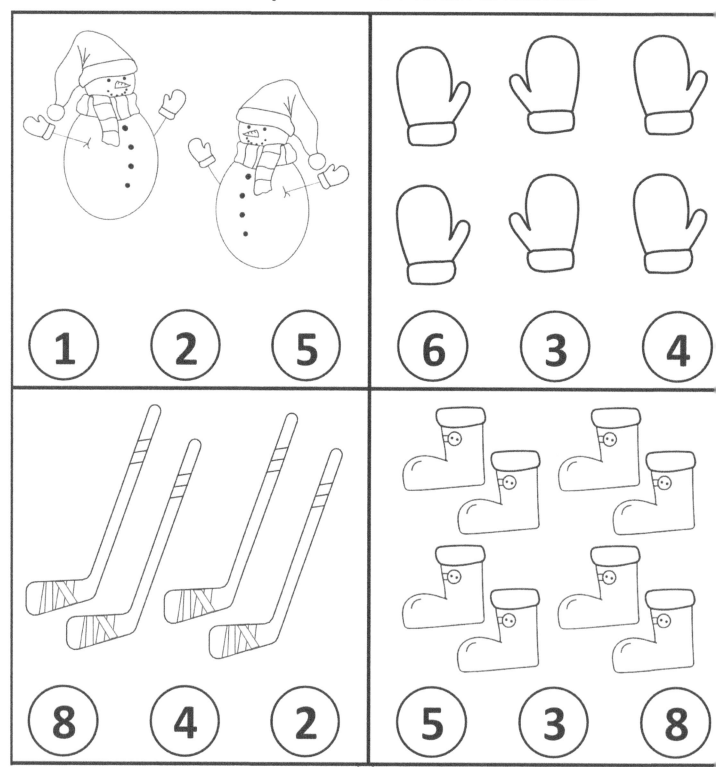

Counting Coins

How much money is in my piggy bank?

_____   _____

_____   _____

Counting Coins

How much money is in my piggy bank?

_____   _____

_____   _____

Dinosaur Color by Number

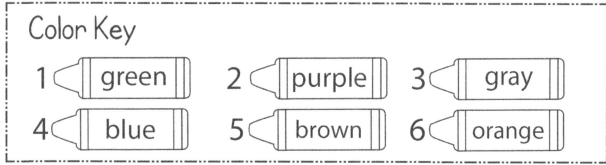

Color Key

1 green   2 purple   3 gray
4 blue   5 brown   6 orange

67

Color by Numbers

1= Orange

2= Brown

3= Dark Brown

4= Yellow

5= Green

Color by Numbers

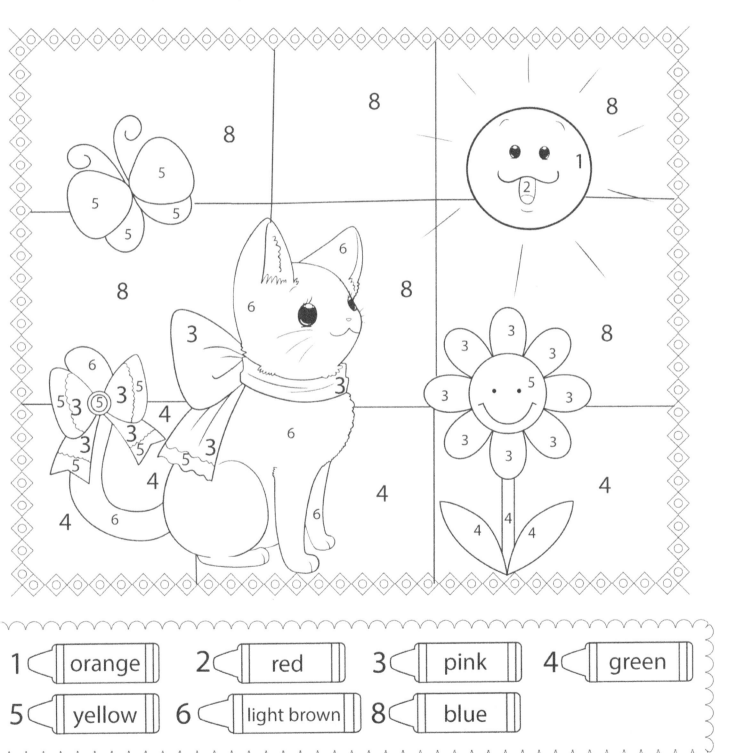

| 1 | orange | 2 | red | 3 | pink | 4 | green |
| 5 | yellow | 6 | light brown | 8 | blue |

Beach Color by Numbers

Color Key

1	brown	2	green	3	white
4	blue	5	gray	6	orange
7	light brown	8	red	9	light blue

70

Color by Numbers

1	orange	2	yellow	3	red	4	blue
5	brown	6	black	7	white	8	green
9	pink						

Shapes

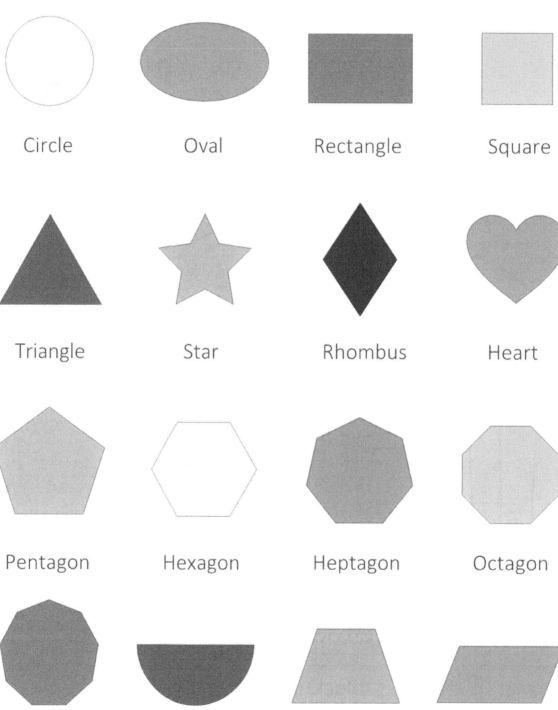

Circle	Oval	Rectangle	Square
Triangle	Star	Rhombus	Heart
Pentagon	Hexagon	Heptagon	Octagon
Nonagon	Semicircle	Trapezoid	Parallelogram

Rectangle

rectangle

Fill in the correct number below.

A rectangle has _____ sides.

A rectangle has _____ corners.

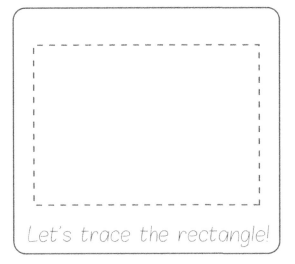

Let's trace the rectangle!

Find the rectangles and color them. How many rectangles do you see? Write the number below.

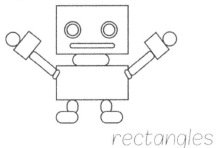

_____ rectangles

Rectangles are hiding in the images. Find and color the rectangles!

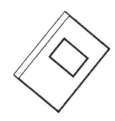

Circle

circle

Fill in the correct number below.

A circle has _____ sides.

A circle has _____ corners.

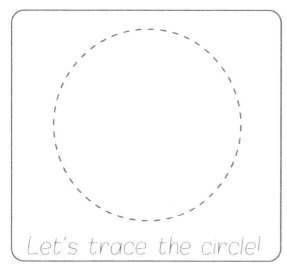

Let's trace the circle!

Find the circles and color them.
How many circles do you see?
Write the number below.

_____ circles

Circles are hiding in the images. Find and color the circles!

Triangle

triangle

Fill in the correct number below.

A triangle has _____ sides.

A triangle has _____ corners.

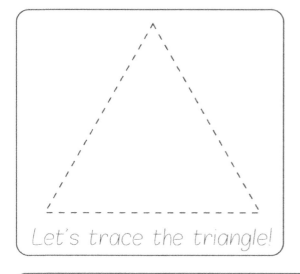

Let's trace the triangle!

Find the triangles and color them. How many triangles do you see? Write the number below.

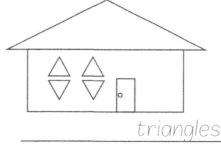

_____ triangles

Triangles are hiding in the images. Find and color the triangles!

  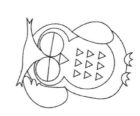

Square

square

Fill in the correct number below.

A square has _____ sides.

A square has _____ corners.

A square has equal sizes.

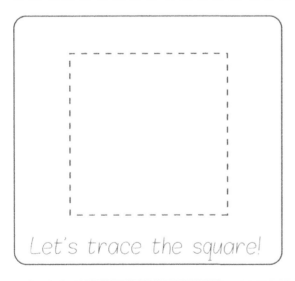

Let's trace the square!

Find the squares and color them. How many squares do you see? Write the number below.

_____ squares

Squares are hiding in the images. Find and color the squares!

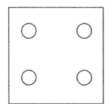

Trace the Shapes

Trapezoid

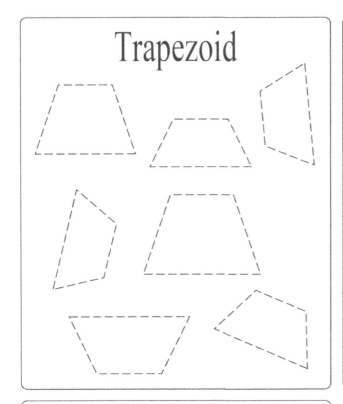

Octagon

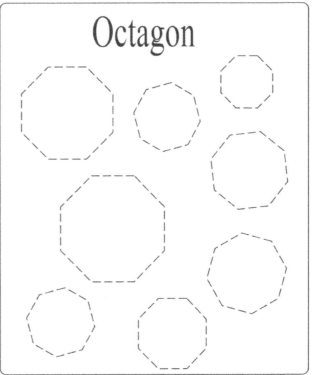

Pentagon

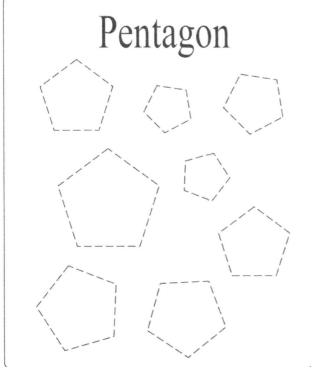

Star

Finish the shapes

The shapes are not complete. Draw the rest of the shapes.

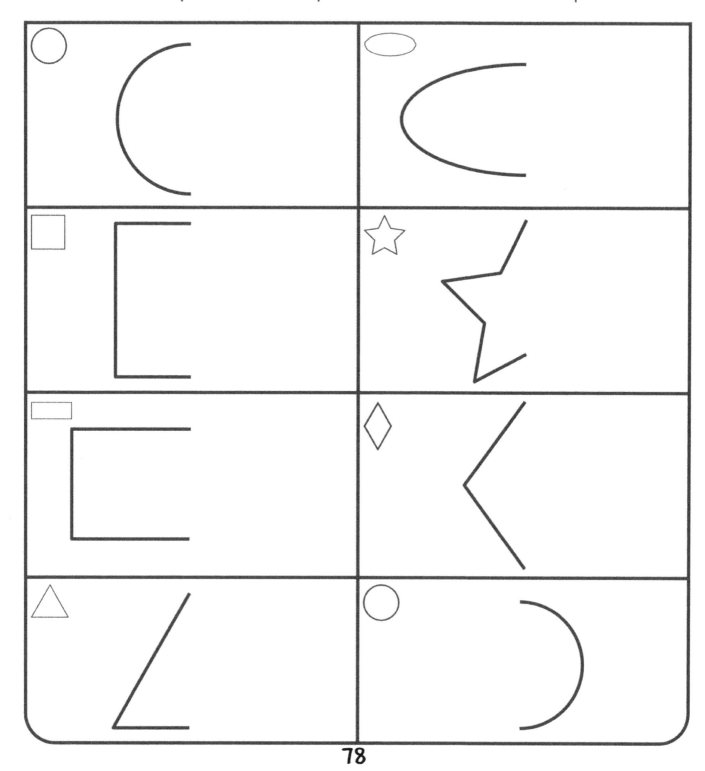

Matching shapes

Directions: Cut and paste the matching shapes.

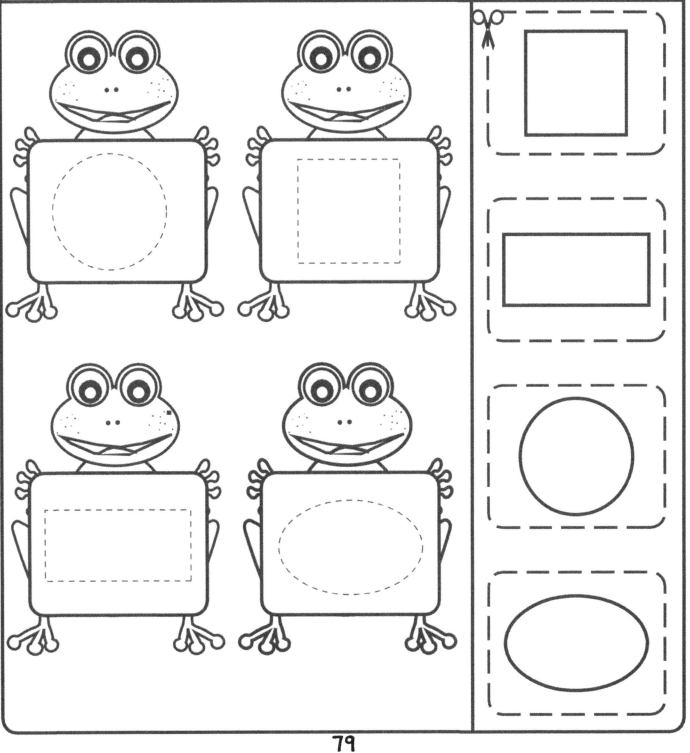

79

Matching shapes

Directions: Cut and paste the matching shapes.

FIND THESE SHAPES:

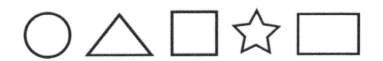

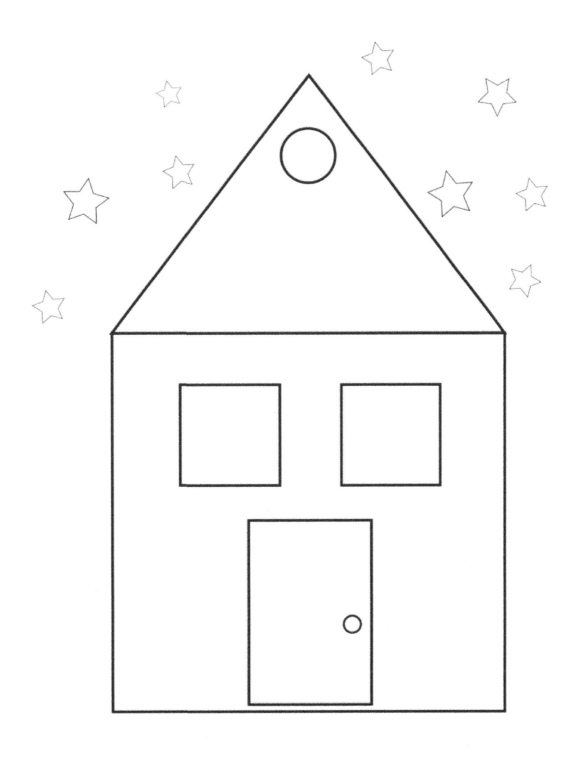

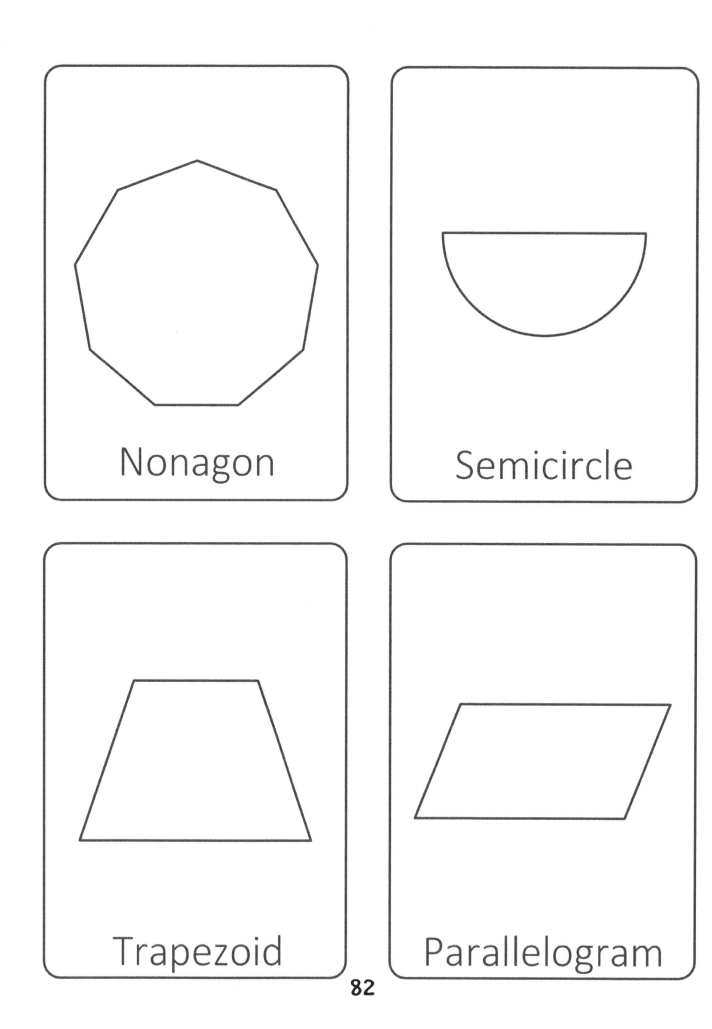

Nonagon

Semicircle

Trapezoid

Parallelogram

MATCH SHAPES

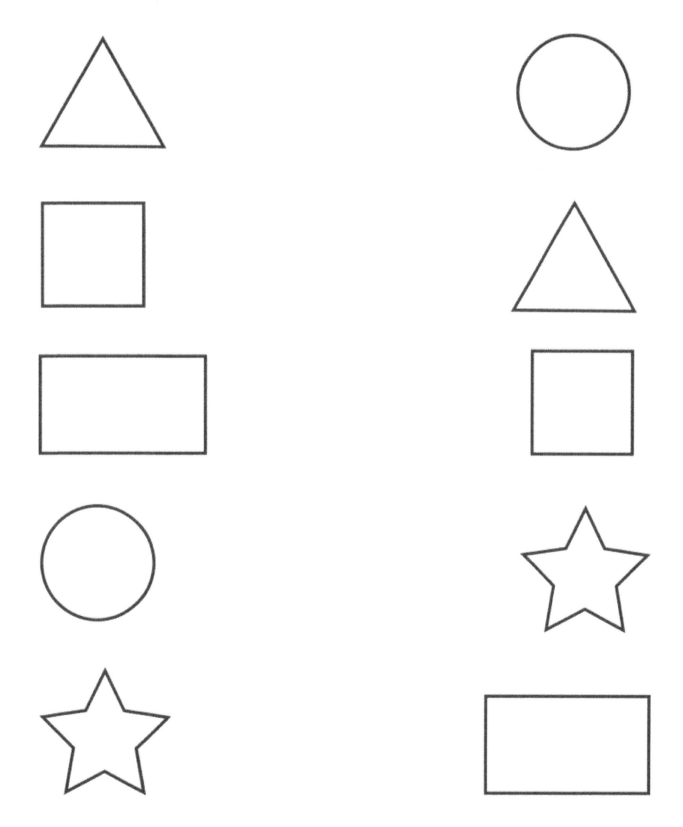

Geometry Patterns

Trace the shapes. Look at each pattern and draw the shape that comes last.

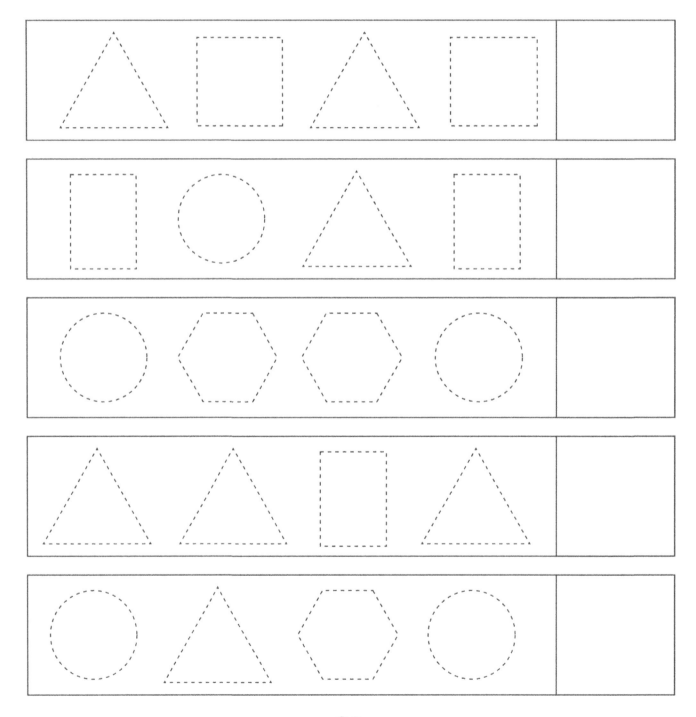

Color in the circles to help the dinosaur find his friend.

85

Paste the shapes

Directions: Cut the shapes, match and paste them on the cats.

Popsicle shapes

Directions: Cut and match popsicles with shapes.

✂ ────────────────────────────────────

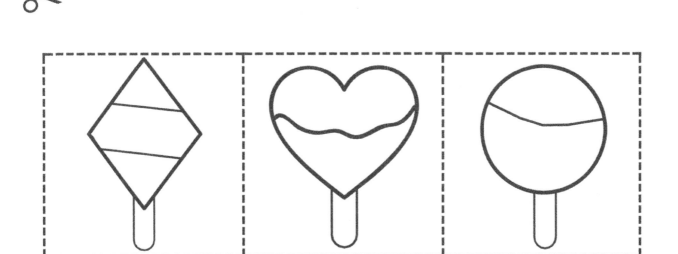

Big or Small?

Circle the BIG PICTURE.

Big or Small?

Circle the small PICTURE.

Which one is the BIGGEST?

Circle the BIGGEST PICTURE.

Which one is the smallest?

Circle the smallest PICTURE.

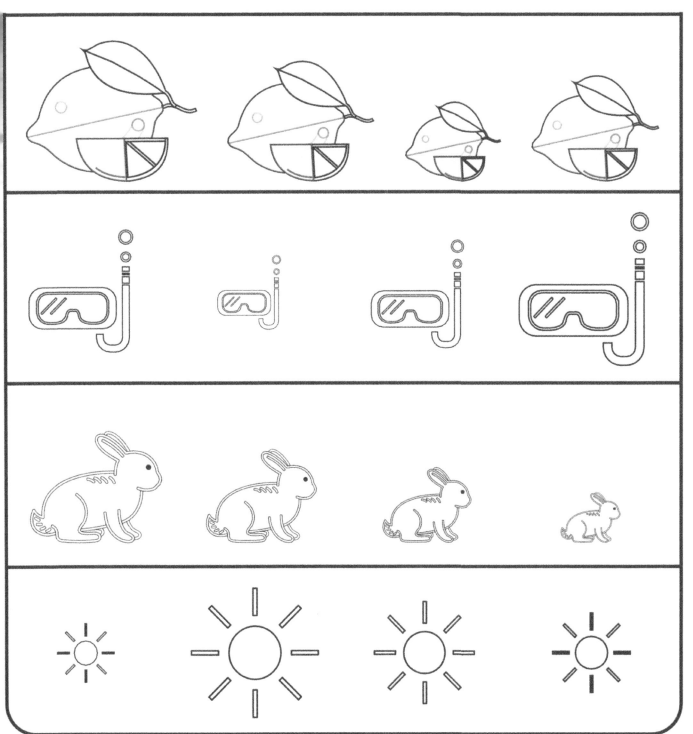

Which one is the BIGGEST?

Directions: Circle the picture that's the biggest.

Which one is the smallest?

Directions: Circle the picture that's the smallest.

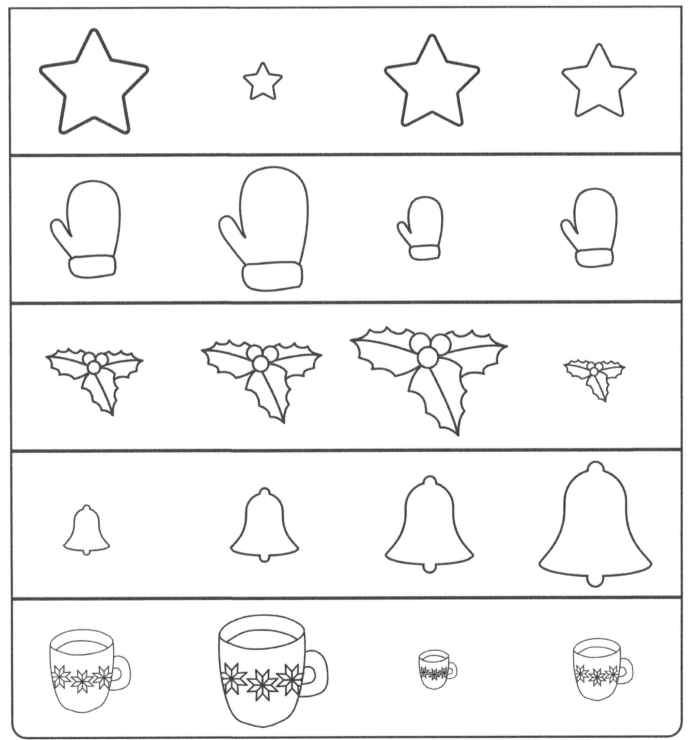

From big to small

Directions: Look at the pictures in each box.
Draw lines in order from the biggest to the smallest picture.

Like this:

Length Measurement

How many blocks equal the length of these sea animals?
Write the answer in each box.

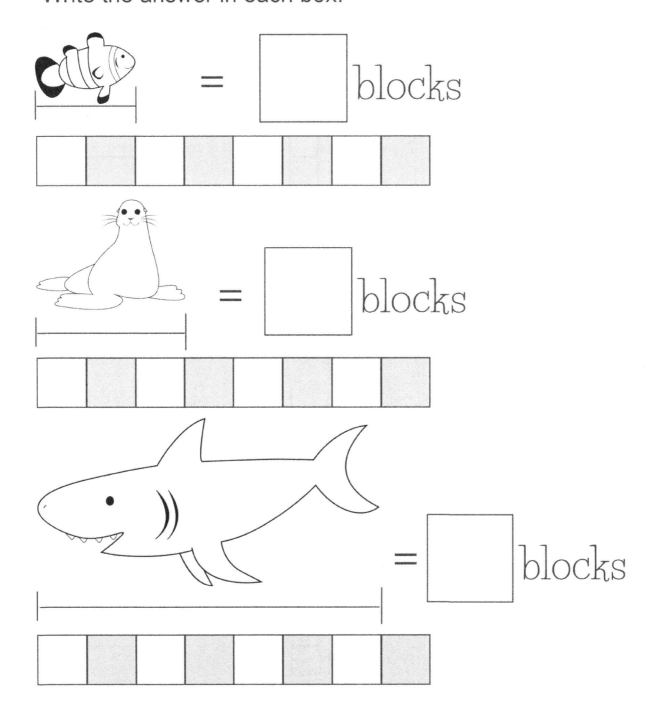

= [ ] blocks

= [ ] blocks

= [ ] blocks

Measuring Height

Measure and record the results below each image. Circle the animals that are taller in each box

blocks

blocks

blocks

blocks

blocks

blocks

blocks

blocks

Measuring Length

Cut out the ruler. Measure the length of the images and record the results.

☐ blocks

☐ blocks

☐ blocks

Short and Tall

Directions: Color the picture that is shorter.

Short and Tall

Directions: Color the picture that is shorter.

Short and Tall

Directions: Color the picture that is shorter.

100

Pattern Activity

Look at the patterns below. Cut out the images and paste the image that comes last in each box.

	paste here
	paste here
	paste here
	paste here

Pattern Activity

Directions: Finish the patterns on each sock.

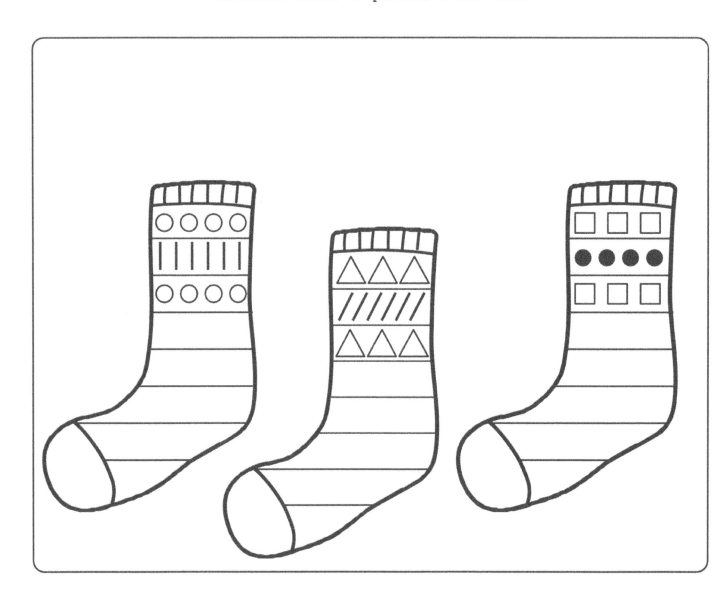

Pattern Activity

What comes next?

Directions: Carefully look at the order of the pictures.
Then draw the rest to finish each row.

Pattern Activity

Which one's different?

Directions: Compare the pictures and circle the one that is different.

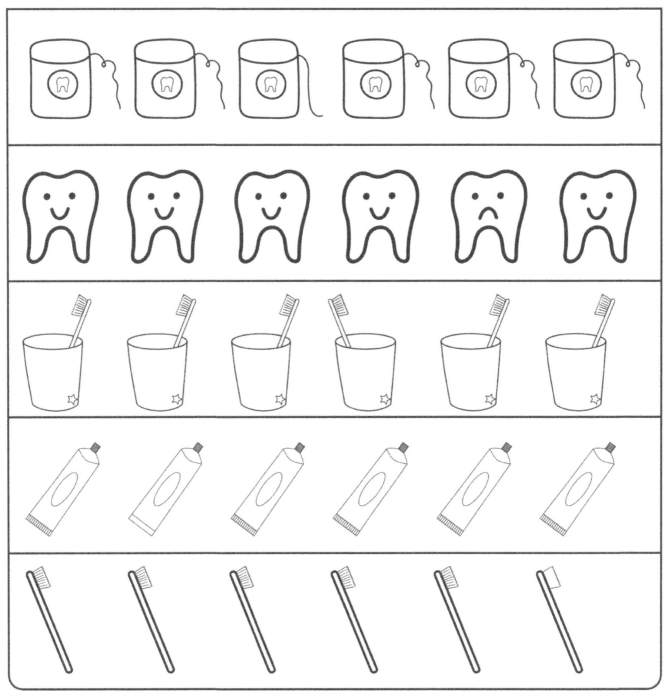

Finish the patterns

Directions: Look at the pictures in each row. Circle the one that comes next.

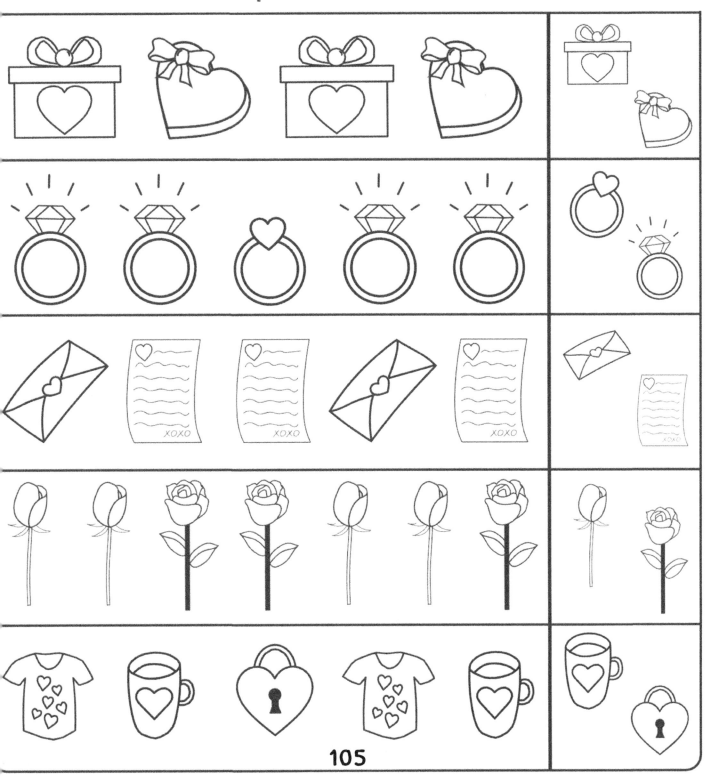

105

Make your own patterns

Directions: Use your favorite colors and make your own patterns!

Same or Different?

Cross out the picture that is different from the rest.

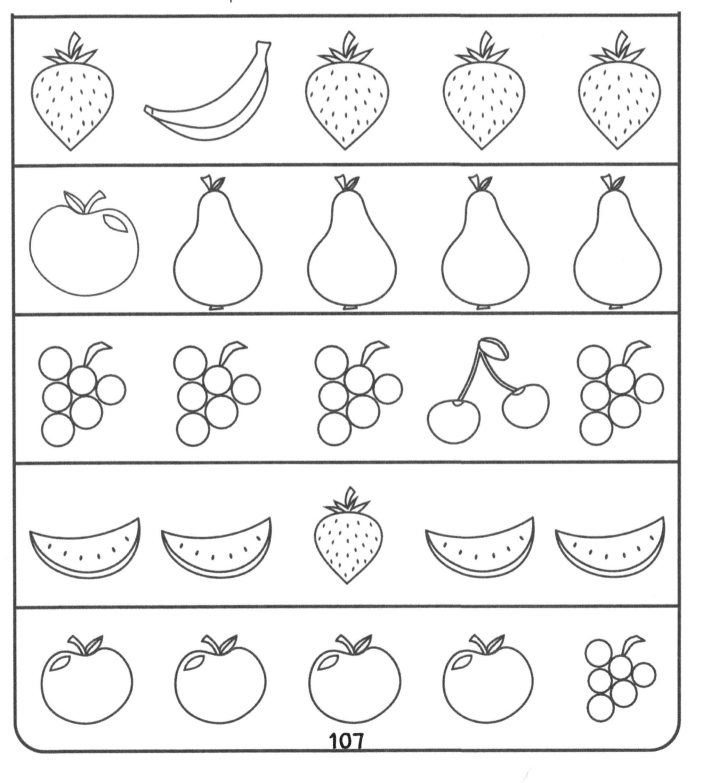

107

What doesn't belong?

Directions: Look at the pictures. Cross out the one that doesn't belong with the rest.

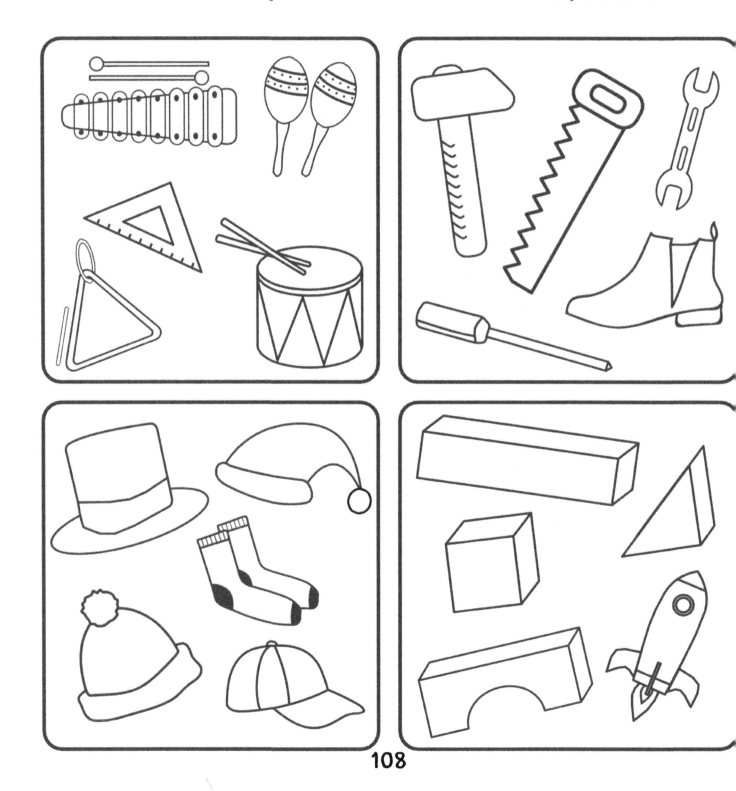

What doesn't belong?

Directions: Look at the pictures. Cross out the one that doesn't belong with the rest.

Same or Different?

Cross out the picture that is different from the rest.

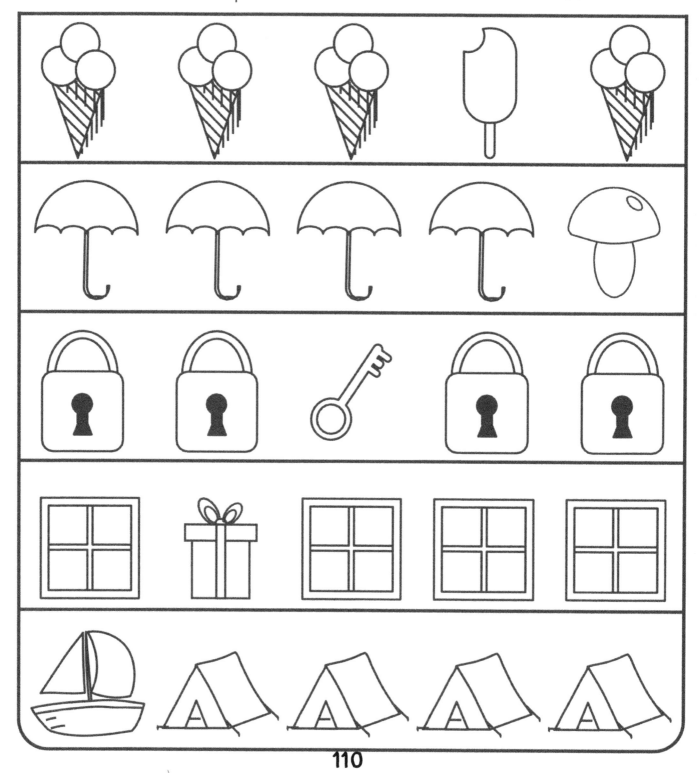

Find my shadow

Directions: Look at the picture in each box. Then find its matching shadow.

Matching pairs

Directions: Draw lines between tea cups that match. Then color them the same way.

Which group has fewer?

Directions: Count the pictures, then write the numbers. Circle the group that has fewer.

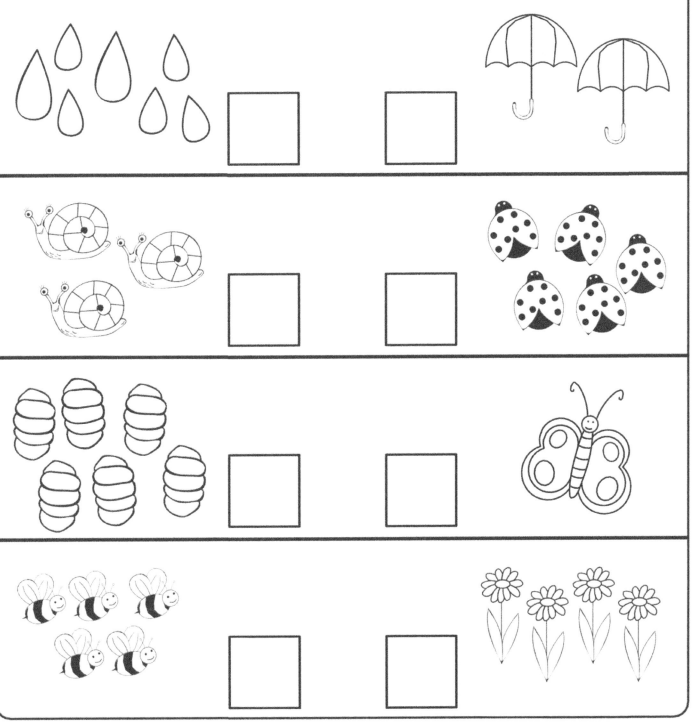

Which group has more?

Directions: Count the pictures, then write the numbers. Circle the group that has more.

Comparing Groups

Count the number of images and write the total number in each box.
Circle the box with more images in each row.

Total Number:_____   Total Number:_____

Total Number:_____   Total Number:_____

Total Number:_____   Total Number:_____

Less or More

Count the number of images and write the total number in each box.
Circle the box with more images in each row.

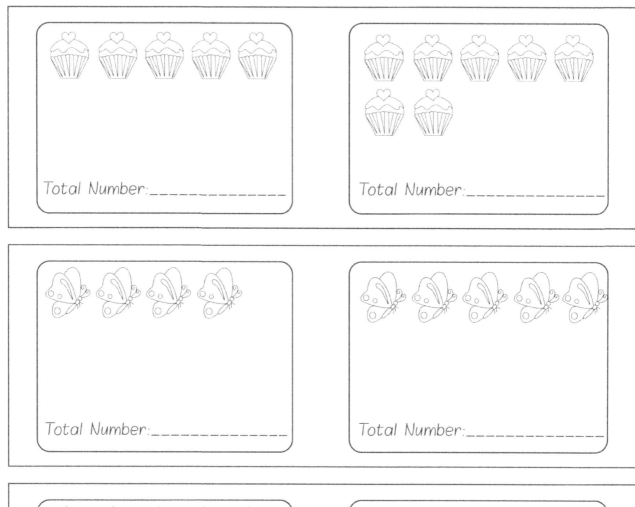

Total Number:_____

Total Number:_____

Total Number:_____

Total Number:_____

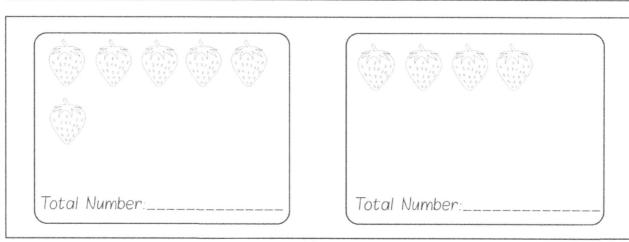

Total Number:_____

Total Number:_____

Comparing Groups

Count the number of images and write the total number in each box.
Circle the box with more images in each row.

Total Number:_____

Total Number:_____

Total Number:_____

Total Number:_____

Total Number:_____

Total Number:_____

Comparing Numbers

Compare the two numbers in each row. Trace more or less to complete each sentence correctly.

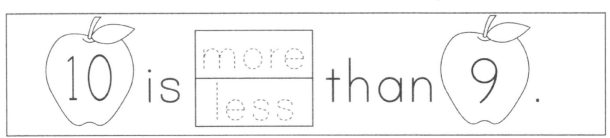

10 is more/less than 9.

3 is more/less than 5.

1 is more/less than 4.

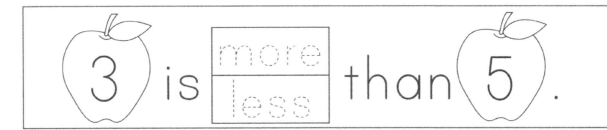

7 is more/less than 2.

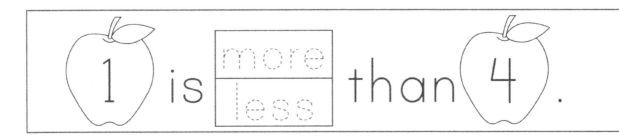

8 is more/less than 6.

Spelling and Coloring

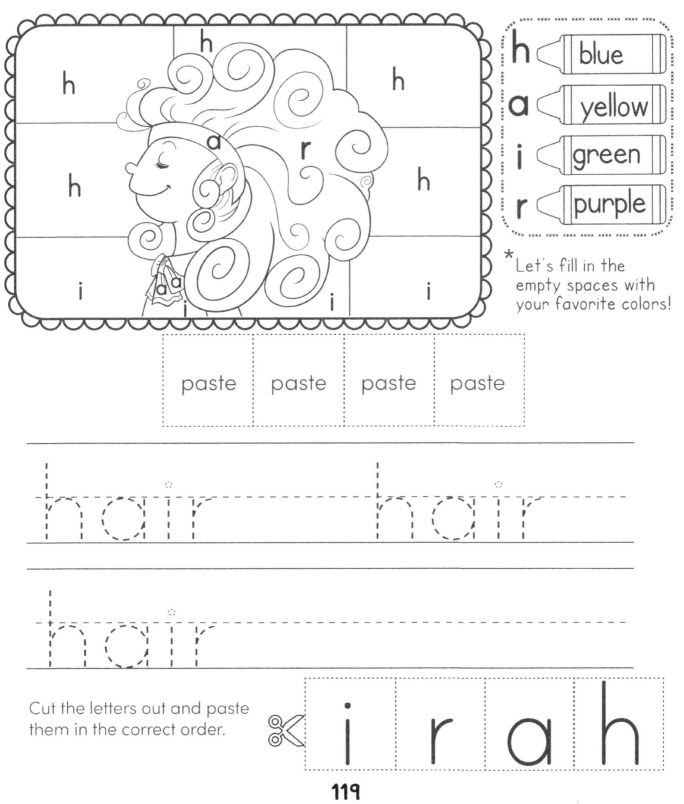

h | blue
a | yellow
i | green
r | purple

*Let's fill in the empty spaces with your favorite colors!

paste | paste | paste | paste

hair   hair

hair

Cut the letters out and paste them in the correct order.

i r a h

Maze

Directions: Help the fruits and vegetables get to the Horn of plenty.

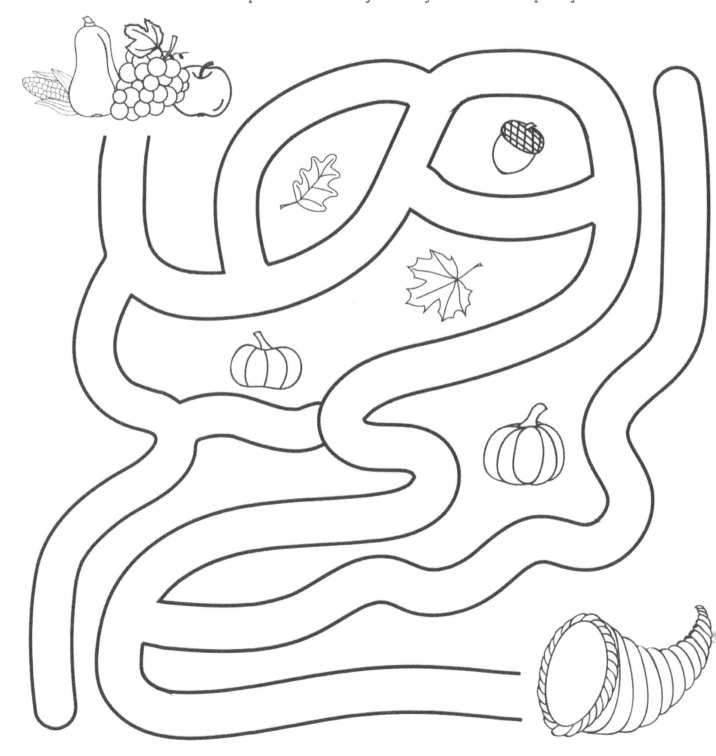

Help the Unicorn Find her Ice Cream

Counting

Directions: Read the numbers. Draw a line to match the numbers with a group.

2 two

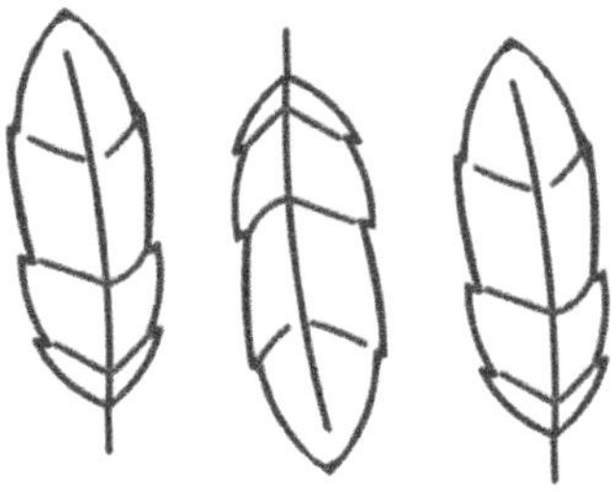

3 three

4 four

5 five

Counting

Directions: Read the numbers. Draw a line to match the numbers with a group.

6 six

9 nine

8 eight

10 ten

7 seven

Lemonade stand letters

Directions: Color only the lemons with letters on them.

Deliver the letters

Directions: Help to put the letters in order for a smooth delivery.
Connect them with a line from A to Z.

Start here →

letters

Directions: Write the missing letters in order.

A   C D

F G   I

   L M   O

   Q   S

U V   Y

Counting

Directions: Count the pictures in each box. Then color the correct number.

Counting

Directions: Count the pictures in each box. Then color the correct number.

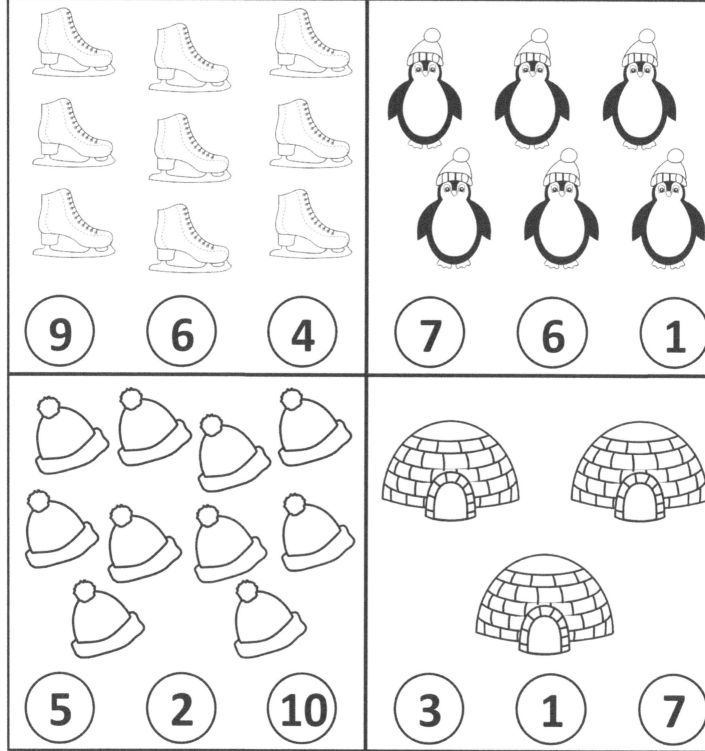

128

Draw the Other side worksheet

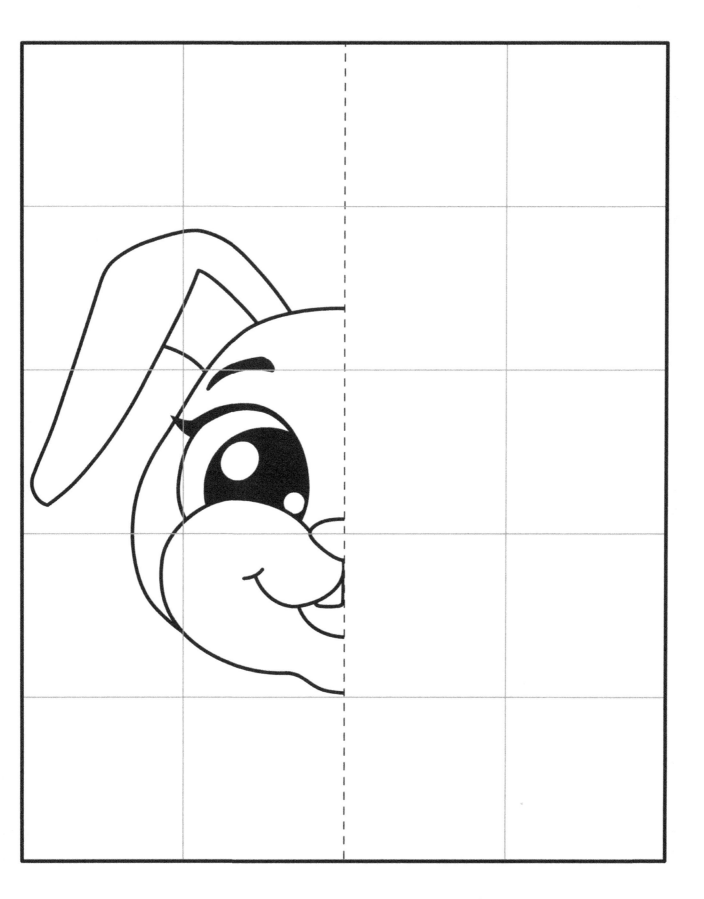

Draw the Other side worksheet

Trace & Color in

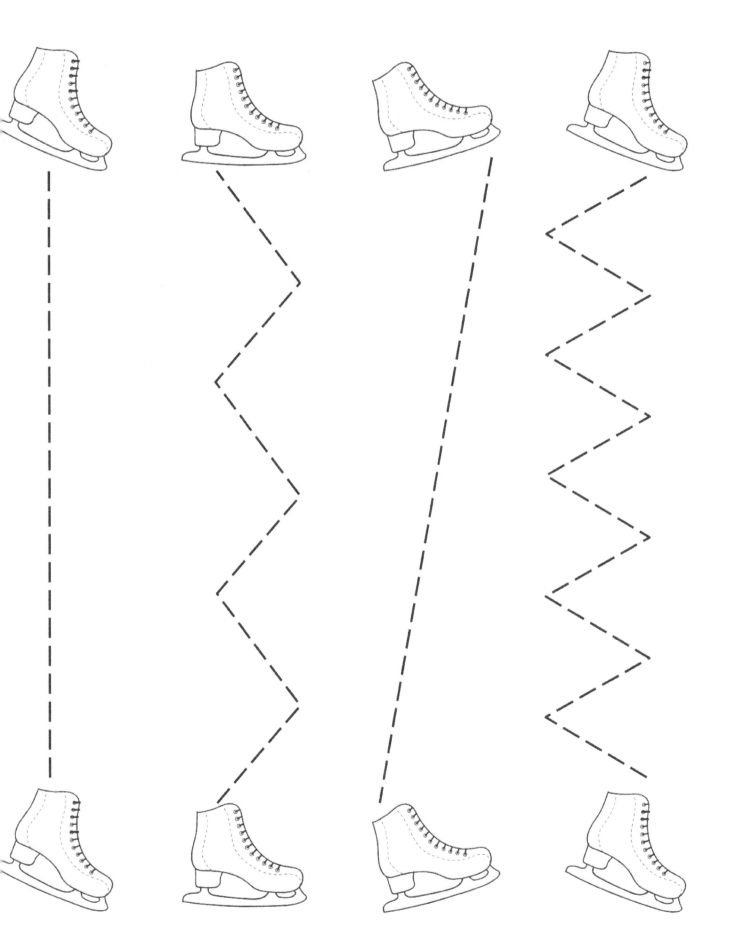

Coloring Page

Triceratops Dinosaur

Color it!

triceratops

Facts About Triceratops

Height: around 10 feet

Weight: about 10 tons

Horns: 3

Teeth: 400 to 800

Food: plants

Let's draw the other half of his face!

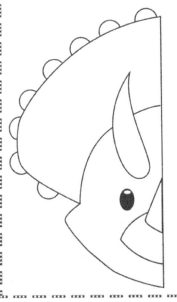

These are my favorites

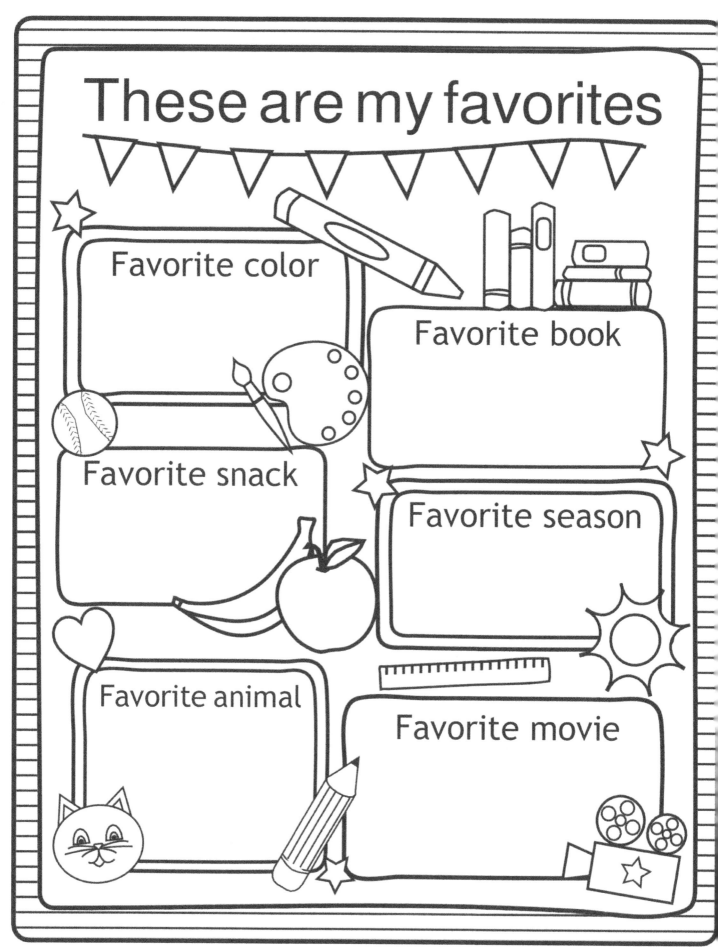

Favorite color

Favorite book

Favorite snack

Favorite season

Favorite animal

Favorite movie

Things that go together

Directions: Circle 2 pictures that belong with the first one.

Things that go together

Directions: Circle 2 pictures that belong with the first one.

What goes together?

Directions: Match the pictures that belong together.

What goes together?

Directions: Match the pictures that belong together.

Let's go to the beach

Directions: Pack the beach bag by coloring only the items we bring to the beach in summer.

Count and color

Directions: Count the pictures, circle the correct number. Then color the five frame.

(acorns)	5 1 3	
(apples)	4 2 5	
(owl)	2 3 1	
(leaves)	3 4 2	
(pears)	5 3 2	

144

Count and color

Directions: Count the pictures, circle the correct number. Then color the five frame.

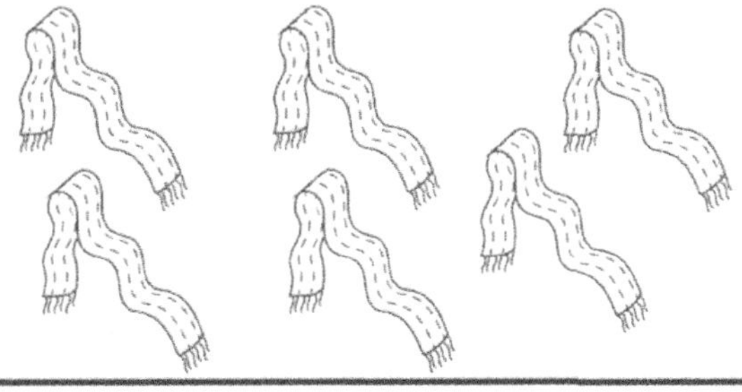

6
10
8

9
7
8

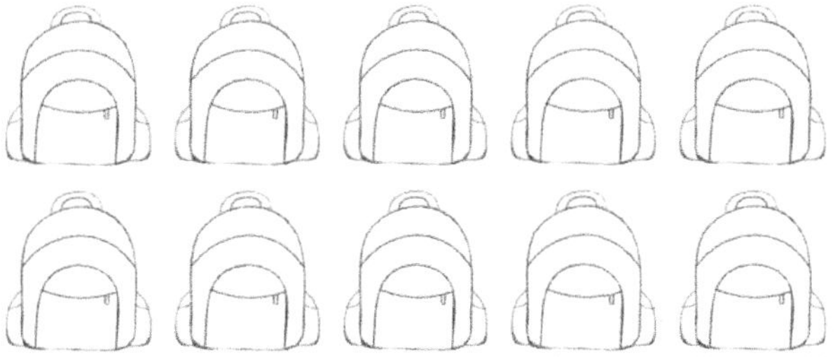

8
6
10

7
6
9

6
8
7

145

Spelling and Coloring

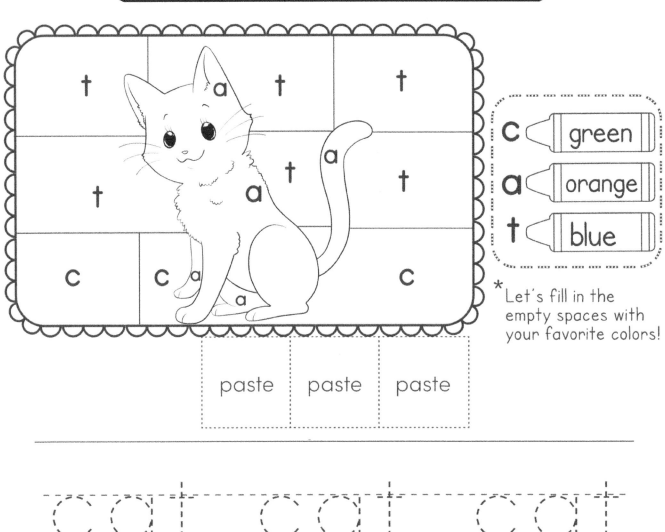

c	green
a	orange
t	blue

paste | paste | paste

*Let's fill in the empty spaces with your favorite colors!

cat cat cat

cat

Cut the letters out and paste them in the correct order.

t c a

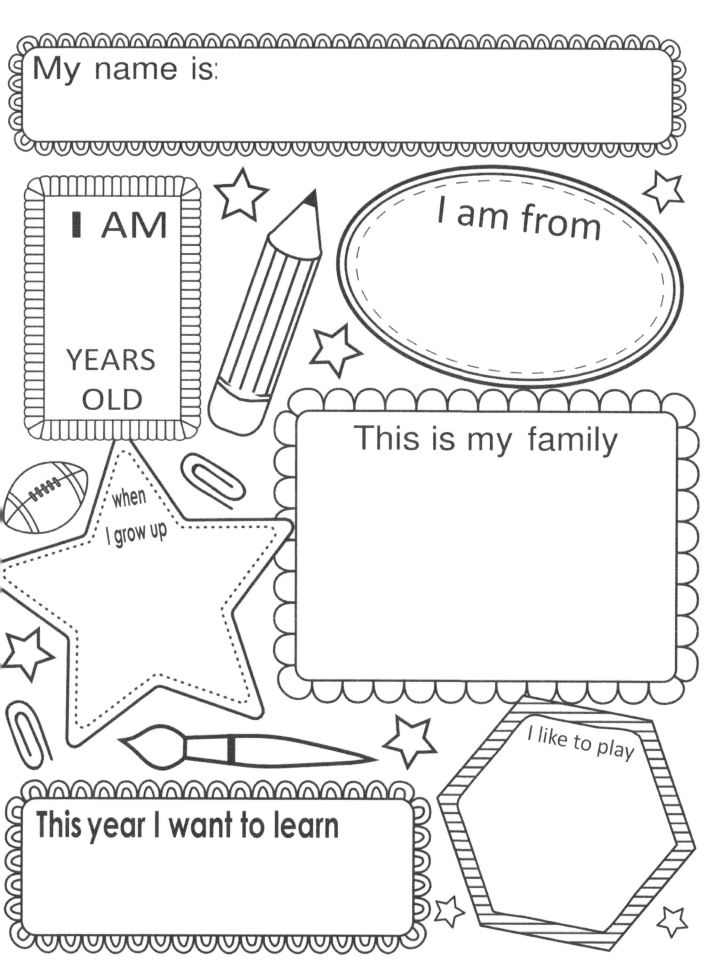

My name is:

I AM

YEARS
OLD

I am from

when
I grow up

This is my family

I like to play

This year I want to learn

147

Preschool
Certificate of Achievement
Awarded to

Proudly presented at

Signed:

Date:

CHECK OUT OUR OTHER BOOKS

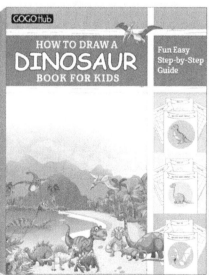

If you liked this book can you please leave us a short review to enable us to write more books for your little one?

CHECK OUT OUR OTHER BOOKS

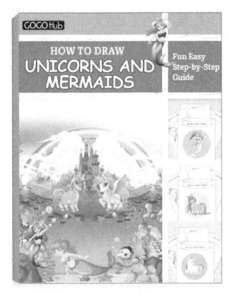

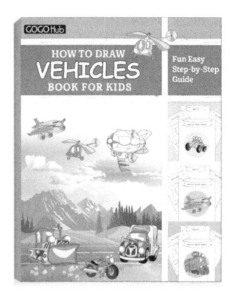

If you liked this book can you please leave us a short review to enable us to write more books for your little one?

A Quick Favor Please?

Thank you so much for choosing our workbook.

Before you go can I ask you for a quick favor?
Would you please leave this workbook a short review, even if it's a few words?

It is quick and painless and will only take a second, promise! Just scroll down our Amazon workbook listing where reviews are, and select "write a customer review".

As a mom myself, I sincerely hope that our workbook has enriched your child's educational journey in supplementing their classroom curriculum. We are a small Californian family business, and our mission is to provide affordable yet helpful, educational products that make life easier on parents.

Marie
GOGO Hub
The Go-to for parents needs
****

www.gogohub.us

Made in United States
Orlando, FL
11 October 2024

52558562R00083